Mama I Sold You

By Thaamir Moerat

Written by Thaamir Moerat in association with Vefa Enver Kitaplar - Türkiye - İstanbul

VE www.vefaenver.com.tr

This book is printed by Tone Media in South Africa

First printing: December 9th 2013

ISBN: 978-0-620-59221-5

Book cover designed by Tauriq Moerat

For more information contact Thaamir Moerat on
thaamir@sellhard.co.za or visit our website at
www.sellhard.co.za

Skype: thaamir.moerat

twitter.com/talktosales

In writing this book I tapped into every sales and life experience I had.

Every moment was worth it...

About the Author

Thaamir Moerat was born in Paarl and matriculated at the prestigious Paarl Boys High in 1997. A varsity drop out, he started his sales career as a telesales agent with no experience and after month one he was the agent of the month. Month two saw him break the record with three hundred sales averaging fifteen a day at a premium of 55 rand per month. Cold calling, referral based sales!

He was immediately promoted to team leader and managed a team of twelve agents averaging 1.2 sales per hour daily. That is 8-10 sales per agent per day.

An opportunity arose in the call centre at an international online gaming company as an inbound entertainment executive dealing with customer queries worldwide. After two months in the call centre, he took the initiative to start prospecting and calling clients to get them spending more.

As the company had no outbound department, he was the only one doing so. He saw the need for an entire department and "pitched" the call centre head to let him recruit a team and start a department from scratch. He gave Thaamir one month to prove to him why.

That month he met and exceeded all sales and inventory targets and his request was granted. One month later, he had a team of 12-14 agents running 24/7 calling around the world and converting players at a rate of 14 per agent per shift.

He quickly developed a reputation as Mr Sales, often working 18 hour shifts 7 days a week.

During this period, he compiled, formatted and edited the training manual (Telemarketing the Entertainer's approach) - a training manual based on selling telephonically in an entertaining manner.

He made his move to online media when the media buyers were struggling to close deals. It was the next logical step as media buying was all about negotiating deals, "negotiating", the brother of "selling". He managed the new media team with great success until his move back to call centre sales as a contracted sales management specialist at a leading 1000 seater call centre company in Cape Town.

Five months later, he joined forces with his previous employers to form a new sales company as a director of call centre sales and operations in Cape Town and Durban.

Here, he compiled, formatted and edited the manual "Mama I Sold You" which became the title of his first book. It started as a training manual designed for training new agents on how to sell all products, specifically to the South African entry level market.

(LSM R2000-R6000)

After month three, the Cape Town call centre broke the record for one of South Africa's leading outsourced financial services products (8000 sales with 60 agents).

This number was achieved frequently thereafter. Two years later, Thaamir was contracted to train 5000 face to face sales reps for the "Commuter Card" project.

Thereafter, Thaamir parted with financial services and is now focused on his sales company, SellHard.co.za and its ventures. He is a critically acclaimed sales trainer used by top companies and this is his first sales book in a series of three.

He is the owner and brains behind products like the GetSmart Card, Stu-D Card, Vvouchers, Al-Isra and CitySleeker. He is the sole owner of The

Fish King Factory shop in Paarl (www.thefishking.co.za).

Thaamir also holds directorship at Vineyards Rugby (Pty) Ltd, and serves on the POBC of the Paarl Boys High old boys union.

In 2013, Thaamir was approached to be the star of a reality show called "The Journey". It follows the lives of the top 12 contestants in the Mr South Africa competition. Thaamir was also the head judge.

He is a lifelong student of the sales game...

Always Hungry. Always Driven.

Thaamir Moerat lives, eats and sleeps sales... He is sales!

"We see training as insurance on our biggest asset - human resources. Find me a company without that insurance that has stopped training its salespeople and I'll target that market and that company and have its business by years end."

David Barcusee of Bergen-Brunswig

Sales & Marketing Management Magazine

After the success of my sales training manuals, my first three books titled "Mama I Sold You", "The Next Best Thing" and "Good Enough Doesn't Cut It" will focus on textbook telephone selling techniques and different face to face sales processes.

It will also be an autobiography of my "Sales Life" and every experience will lead to some sort of sales lesson.

If you are about to read this book and have an interest in investing in your sales health you are on the right path. To fully appreciate my "sales autobiography" you will need to bear in mind that this is just the first of an ongoing series of sales training books, three of which will complete this series, as my sales journey will never end... I will never stop learning.

A true salesman is a lifelong student. Always learning, always seeking new ways to refine the art of selling.

Remember, formal education will make you a living.

Sales education will make you a fortune!

The first question you need to ask yourself is: Why did you choose sales as a career? One of the answers to this question is probably that you like talking to people.

It is unlikely that you would have chosen this field if you were an introvert or a very shy person.

Sales is a process, not a goofy technique or gimmick. Salesmen must be able to communicate often and with a wide variety of people.

Chances are that you meet this requirement.

However, even if you are good at conversations, and you are at ease when speaking to people, you will need to refine certain oral skills for the communication that is going to be part of your job.

Always remember that effective communication is the key to success!

You will be taught these skills throughout this book. I have based my training mostly on my experience. It will equip you with skills that will enable you to adjust to the client and tell him the "story" exactly the way he wants to hear it.

My folks always say that I should've stayed in the entertainment industry. I say we are in the entertainment industry!

As sales agents we are entertainers. Our body language, tone of voice and speaking skills should be used to "entertain" people into making the decisions that we want them to in order to make that sales pitch successful.

As sales professionals, we are not Customer Service Representatives. Yet if you want to truly be customer focused, then stop being so bloody nice!

Be relentless, be aggressive! "There is no such thing as a "No" sale call. A sale is made on every call or pitch you make. Either you sell the client your product or he sells you a reason he can't buy. Either way a sale is made, the only question is who is going to close? You or him?"

Mind you, I'm not talking about being rude, mean or over aggressive to clients. Instead, your job starting today is to help potential clients figure out how to improve their lives by taking up your offer or buying your product.

That means that you must always strive to set the scene to get them buying. Because that's what winning is to us! The more people purchasing, the more we gain.

TOC

Chapter 1: Birth of a Salesman

"The two most important days in your life are the day you were born, and the day you find out why."

Mark Twain

"Got to get this job!" That was the only thing that went through my mind as I was sitting in my car. I knew nothing about sales. I knew nothing about call centre. I knew nothing about what I was about to do.

All I knew was that I was hungry, literally and figuratively and that I didn't have money to get home and I needed this. It was now or never. I remember walking up the stairs with my CV in my hand thinking "I don't have any experience".

Why would they care wasting time on me? Why would they even consider me? All I knew was that this was it. It was now or never! So I went for it.

In my 7000 Rand Hugo Boss suit which my dad had bought for me before he went bust (more on that later), no money in my pocket, no food in my stomach and no petrol in my tank, I had no choice but to go for it.

This was my time! The manager at the Call Centre was an Afrikaans guy. Big, strong and very domineering, almost scary.

He looked at me and said: "Mr Armani suit are you at the right place?" I told him that it was actually a Hugo Boss suit which my dad bought for me before he lost everything. He smirked and said: "Let me see your CV". I gave it to him and there was nothing in it related to sales except for some promotional work I did.

Up until that time all I did was model, dance and some promotion work. He shook my hand and said they would call me but I knew that they wouldn't. That was the first time I sold myself hard. I put it all out there and told him that I had no money to get home and I would be sleeping in my car that night and probably the next few nights after that. So I wasn't going anywhere. I told him that I needed this job and if he taught me, I could do it.

11

Being Danjoe he just looked at me and said: "Step into my office." He said: "Sit down and tell me your story" and at that moment I was so emotionally drained I just broke down and cried. I told him my story and said that I needed this job, I've nowhere else to go and he must give me the opportunity and not pay me until I've proven myself. He stood up opened his drawer and gave me the product manual for a 6 in 1 plan.

He said to me: "Here's the product. Show me you can make a sale today and you can come back tomorrow." Now the product was really complicated. It was some sort of funeral cover and HIV protection plan going for

49 Rand per month. It also had a few assist benefits like repatriation, medical and road side assistance.

I studied the product for an hour and started shadowing the call centre agents on the floor. This was my first experience of a sales call centre and it was all so overwhelming and new to me. I was in awe of these fearless "dogs", "wolves"... "HUNTERS"!

Later in my career as I grew in my profession I read a book called "Sales Dogs" by Blair Singer. Now if you know call centres it is full of characters and this was the first day I saw the different breeds of sales dogs. There are five in total and every sales call centre has them. Blair Singer describes them perfectly!

Anybody can sell but only if you are trained properly.

According to Robert Kiyosaki's Rich Dad Sales Advisor, Blair Singer, salespeople and dogs train the same way.

Think about it, dogs would come up to you, drop a stick or a ball at your feet a thousand times, take any rejection in the universe and would still drop the same object at your feet hoping that you'll throw it for them.

Great training is also the main reason why great dogs can hunt, just like how great salespeople are able to sum up their prospects, see who's interested in buying and who is not, and close the deal successfully.

Based on this principle, Blair developed a unique profiling system that compares the different breeds of dogs to the different types of sales personalities.

Just like the five breeds of Sales Dogs, there are five types of salespeople. If you want to put a lot more cash into your pocket, you have to learn to identify the breed of Sales Dog that you are so that you are better aware of your weaknesses and can play to your natural talents.

So take a couple of minutes to match your personality against the five types of Sales Dogs below and see which breed fits you the best!

The following is an extract from Blair Singers book "Sales Dogs"

Pitbull

The most aggressive and probably the most stereotyped salesperson is the Pitbull.

They will attack with a ferocity, aggression and tenacity that is both awe inspiring and terrifying. All they need is a pant cuff to latch on to and they NEVER let go.

Their intensity is rivalled only by their lack of fear. They are the classic thick–skinned, aggressive salesperson. Closing and objection handling is breakfast for this champion.

The Pitbulls success comes from sheer power and fearlessness. They will make more calls, field more rejections and keep on selling more than any other breed, even when they should really back off.

Golden Retriever

Everyones favourite is the Golden Retriever. The typical Retriever sells by providing extraordinary customer service and they will go to great lengths to grant favours for their customers.

The wise Retriever is successful because they know that by continually taking care of prospects, clients and members of their team, customers will keep coming back and the referrals will flow. Long-term service is the key.

Poodle

Poodles are highly intelligent and highly conscious of their appearance. They always look good and will never consider getting their paws dirty over chasing some stupid stick into the river and into the mud.

They know the latest trends and are incredibly well connected. In fact, they probably have the most extensive and exclusive network of any of the breeds!

Poodles also love to speak in front of groups and be the centre of attention. And it is this natural ability to articulate a message that makes Poodles large sums of money.

Chihuahua

Chihuahuas are technical wizards. Their product knowledge and understanding of processes is astounding. When they have a point to be made, they are insistent about driving their point home.

Don't ever get a Chihuahua started on a subject they are passionate about. They won't just talk, they will shout, scream, rant and rave a mile a minute.

Prospects can only be amazed and impressed with the incredible exhibition of passion, emotion and technical detail.

Whilst the Chihuahua is not always the best lap dog, it's the breed you want on your team when digging up data and putting together vital presentations. With boundless energy, Chihuahuas can pull off all-nighters better than any other breed.

Bassett Hound

The classic of all classics is the faithful Bassett Hound. This companion will stick by you through thick and thin. You may try to chase this dog away, yet it would always come back.

When they sell, they have that distinctively humble approach that is designed to drive an arrow deep into your heart. If their pathetic look doesn't get you and begging doesn't work, beware! You may be about to experience Plan B - the picture of their family and stories about having to pay for braces, bicycles and ballet classes!

They will do anything to solicit your sympathy and their favourite word is "Please?" – "Please buy from me", or "Please give me an answer today".

I recommend that you buy and read this book by Blair Singer titled "Sales Dogs"!

After watching all these Sales Dogs in action and taking notes I felt ready to get on to the phone. My first call a guy answered and all I did was froze! I was so afraid of speaking, something that I did so well.

I realised at that moment that being good at conversation and actually "talking to sell" is SO different! Sales is a process after all.

I didn't know how to open. Opening is the most important part of the call. You have exactly ten seconds when you meet your prospect to get him interested or to have him hang up. I would suggest that you write down your opening and learn it like a parrot. Everything else in your call should be a response to your prospects' questions, but your opening should be scripted and perfected.

Do your opening well, show class, have pride and display character and the sales process takes care of itself.

Always make sure that your product knowledge is good before making a call.

I don't believe in formal call scripts for sales agents but one should have a guideline written down, a step by step format for the conversation that you need to "control" and lead towards your "call goal" in making the call a success. It is very unprofessional to say "uhm" during the call.

It makes you sound unintelligent and the prospect will feel that you are wasting their time.

Please, at all times avoid saying anything that will make the prospect feel that you do not know what you are talking about. Use a transition. (Explained in chapter 5)

Opening

The only objective of your telesales opening is to entice curiosity and interest. Nothing else! You need to get your prospect to willingly and enthusiastically move to the questioning. The more questions you get your prospect to ask the better chances you have in closing the deal. A quiet prospect is an uninterested and dead prospect!

You must answer, "What's in it for me?" for the listener, or they will immediately begin the process of trying to get rid of you.

You are only looking for one decision in your opening. That is for the customer to decide to continue speaking with you. That's it! You can't close in the first few seconds of a call so all you are looking for is a start, a start to your well prepared sales pitch.

When calling current clients, don't start the call with, "I was just calling people", clients want to feel like they're the only person you're calling, not just one of the masses from a list of compiled names on your database.

For example, "Because you are one of our most valuable customers, it is of the utmost importance that I called you personally and made sure that you will" or "As a leading customer".

The purpose for your opening is to put your listener in a positive state of mind and ease him up to you. Secondly, to effectively transition you to the next part of the call namely the conversation and the questioning. You don't want to make a presentation if they're not ready yet. You don't want to sell hard if they are not ready for it.

Write out your openings. I already said this and I can't stress it enough!

Yes, script them word for word. Everything else you'll say on the call is in response to what your client has to say, but the opening must be prepared and studied like a parrot. This way you know it will work.

I had the same opening for every call when I was on the phones many years ago and one day a colleague of mine asked me if I did not get bored of that same line.

My answer was that every client hears it for the first time and laughs so if it works for me, why change it.

Try not to sound like you're working from a prepared opening though. You hate it when a robot sound-alike calls you at home and reads poorly from scripts, so don't you become one of those boring robots!

Look at your opening as if you were the person hearing it. If it doesn't get you interested and if it doesn't excite you, how in the world could it get the attention of your prospects? Change it and start over.

When editing your opening, scrutinise every word and idea over and over before using it.

Ask yourself this question, "Is this adding to the effectiveness of the opening or not?" If not, delete it or reword it. Be relentless in your editing. It is better for you to rip it apart than your prospect.

Don't apologise for taking someones' time at the beginning of a call. It diminishes your importance.

When someone calls me and says: "Sorry to bother you",   I immediately brace myself for a long and boring sales call.

For example, consider the caller who says: "I know you're busy, and I'm sorry for interrupting... I'll just take a few seconds of your time and here's why I'm calling".

Stop it right there!

Think about what you are really offering. Think about your product or service. You have something of value that will help make this persons life more entertaining or exciting depending on the product or service you are offering.

You need to present that feeling with conviction. If you're not sold on your importance, they certainly won't be.

"Act as if"

Later in chapter six, I mention my favourite sales movies but this scene with Ben Affleck, the "Act as if" scene has to get mentioned now! I will

18

say it again! **If you're not sold on your importance, they certainly won't be.**

PG 18: "**Jim Young:** There's an important phrase that we use here, and think it's time that you all learned it. Act as if. You understand what that means? Act as if you are the f.....g President of this firm. Act as if you got a 9 inch c...k. Okay? Act as if."

Start your calls well, and the rest becomes easier.

Opening statements that build resistance and not interest:

Within the first ten seconds, you create one of two emotions within the person you're speaking to: Resistance or interest. Nothing Else!

Unfortunately, most callers create resistance and that results in what they perceive as morale killing rejection, along with an early exit from the phone call.

Here's what I heard a guy say: "We deal with selling insurance and I'd like to talk to you about that"

The listener then thinks "So what pal? Why should I listen to you?"

Here's another one: "I sent you an e-mail and was wondering if you got it?"

So what if they did! What are they supposed to say?   "Oh yes so glad you called! I was thinking about your   e-mail all weekend!"

Yeah right, no chance...

What should you say in the beginning of your call?

Introduce yourself and your organisation clearly, entice curiosity with a benefit that will get their attention immediately, get them involved in conversation and get them asking questions.

Be sure that you project all the confidence and believability in the world when you state your price, answer all those tough questions and ask for their commitment or their business.

Sending unnecessary paperwork:

When you get the "send me an e-mail or some paperwork" request, be certain the person is a legitimate prospect and not someone that is just trying to get rid of you.

It's better to get the "No" word now, rather than later, after you've already invested lots of money and lots of your precious time. If you hear the request early in the call, I suggest you respond with:

"I'll be happy to send you information. So that I can conclude what would apply best in your situation, let me ask you a few more questions first."

If the request comes later, after you've already made the presentation, say:

"I'll be happy to send you something that summarizes what we discussed on this call. Let me ask you this though, if you like what you see and I know you will,   I'm assuming we will be able to do business together?"

Getting through to your decision maker:

Screeners are some of the most important people you'll ever talk to. After all, they hold the key to the decision makers' door.

There's one simple way you can ensure you'll get through to more decision makers.

Let them know why the boss would be better off by speaking with you. Show them why you are important.

A few examples of this:

"…I work for a company that… and to determine if this is something he'd like to take a look at, I'd like to speak with him about his plans regarding…"

Consider calling Sandy, Richards' PA:

"You probably work closely with Mr De Waal and I bet that you help him with decisions time and again. There might be some information you can help me with first."

Don't be stalled by the:

"Just send any information you have, request"

Respond with something like:

"As a matter of fact Sandy, one of my reasons for calling is to eventually send something to Mr De Waal, but I wouldn't want to waste his time sending a lengthy email that didn't apply to his situation. So what I'd like to do is ask you some questions regarding…"

For call backs dealing with screeners:

"Richard and I had agreed to speak again today. We had a conversation about this last week"

What to do when they say: "Make it quick".

People say these statements only as a natural resistant defence mechanism as it gets rid of sales people who self destruct under pressure.

"That's fine, unless of course after a few minutes you'd like me to continue?"

Or

"If you don't like what I am going to say, then feel free to end the call at anytime!"

The opening is just the beginning of the grand plan. Be certain you know where you're headed next, and what questions you'll ask.

I didn't know any of these opening techniques back then. I thought that sales was just a goofy technique and a gimmick. I faced rejection all day long. Call after call people were just hanging up on me.

I put the phone down and decided to go and listen to the top agent on the floor who called himself Mr Fabulous. This guy thought he was in The Matrix. It was in the heart of summer, he was wearing a black coat, boots and dark shades. He had this arrogance about himself, almost untouchable.

When I stepped into his "territory", he looked down at me and said: "Welcome to The Matrix, I am Neo, and there can be only one!"

It was a bit weird seeing that "There can be only one" was the slogan to the Highlander movies and The Matrix was just "The One"!

Nevertheless, I decided that I needed to be friends with this guy. I had 20 Rand in my pocket and it was almost lunch time. So I offered to buy him a chip roll as that was all I could afford.

He accepted and during that lunch break he helped me with my pitch. I came back after lunch with a renewed confidence ready to make ten sales.

Four hours and two hundred calls later I still had zero on the board and everyone was about to leave but I wasn't. As having spent most of my money on Mr Fabulous, I took my last 5 Rand, I went to the shop downstairs and bought myself six rolls and a black coffee.

I went back to my work station and got busy again. Rejection after rejection, my spirit kept sinking and Danjoe was just sitting there and watching me until the breakthrough came.

I called this lady in the Eastern Cape Township, 'Motherwell'.

Her name was Destiny, but she told me to call her Mama.

That call lasted an hour and I tried everything just to get her to buy but she wouldn't budge! At that moment I asked her what she was doing.

She told me that she was sitting at a window watching her youngest son, Shapping, playing football in the street with his friends. That was when something clicked in my mind.

As I was selling insurance for HIV, I decided to focus on Shapping and sold her on all her insecurities.

After that call, at that moment, I sat back in my chair and told myself I can do this. I had made my first sale and it felt exhilarating. I had never felt so good in my life before and I was hungry to have this feeling again.

I thought to myself "Mama I Sold You" and a salesman was born.

In chapter eight I go into detail about my experience of making my first real sale.

For those of you who know me, this book has been six years in the making. I just needed to build up enough experience and find the perfect time to launch my series.

There are so many sales trainers and motivational speakers out there, but how many of them are really practising what they preach?

I purposefully delayed the publishing of this book for a time in my life that I can say that I am practising what I preach!

That moment I decided that this is what I was going to be doing. This was my calling!

Comments by Vefa Enver:

"He shook my hand and said they would call me but I knew that they wouldn't.

That was the first time I sold myself hard. I put it all out there and told him that I had no money to get home and I would be sleeping in my car that night and probably the next few nights after that. So I wasn't going anywhere.

I told him that I needed this job and if he taught me I could do it.

Being Danjoe he just looked at me and said: "Step into my office." He said: "Sit down and tell me your story" and at that moment I was so emotionally drained I just broke down and cried."

The first time I heard this story I asked myself if I could play the part. They say real freedom comes when you have nothing else to lose. Maybe it is why Thaamir was so persistent and did not take "No" for an answer.

One shot which he could not afford missing... Still, if I was in his shoes would I do the same thing? Imagining the situation, I created various scenes in my head and unfortunately the answer is "No".

I have to confess that I would hand the guy my CV, turn my back and walk away with my head held high instead of staying there and making him understand why I desperately needed this job.

He would either call me back in a few months or never. Most of us confuse pride with the fear of losing. Your desire to succeed should be greater than your fear of losing.

Many people miss opportunities because they are too scared of rejection or to step out of their comfort zone. Somehow ironically anything can be turned into motivation, even fear itself.

As Larry Ellison said: "Great achievers are driven not so much by the pursuit of success but by the fear of failure."

Which side of this debate you relate to, I don't know, but from my point of view, Thaamir is a brilliant example of the latter.

Chapter 2: Lessons from "Rich Dad Poor Dad"

"You're only poor if you give up. The most important thing is that you did something. Most people only talk and dream of getting rich. You've done something."

Robert T. Kiyosaki

I was born in a town called Paarl in the Western Cape Province of South Africa. My mum always told the story of the riots that were happening in my hometown and across the country the day she went into labour. If you know the history of South Africa, the 16th of June is Youth Day. It is the day that African school kids in Soweto decided to protest against being taught in Afrikaans. They decided to march in the streets of Soweto and the government opened fire on them. It was a bloodbath.

Every year on June 16th our country was in turmoil. My mother always said that's why I am what I am.

I don't remember much about my early years. All I remember is always being happy as my father never said no and we got everything we wanted. Being the second eldest in a family of five boys meant that I was always looked up to by three younger brothers and at an early age I felt a sense of responsibility.

My father inherited the fishing business from his father which his father inherited from his father. The Moerats' have been businessmen since the first one set sail from France two centuries ago. The Moerat surname is as synonymous in Paarl with the fishing trade as it is with rugby. I am lucky to carry on with the legacy of both "The Fish King" and "Vineyards Rugby Club".

I love this quote by John Ruskin when thinking of the fishing trade and our beloved Vineyards Rugby club:

"When we build, let us think that we build forever. Let it not be for present delight or for present use alone. Let it be such work as our descendents will thank us for; and let us think, as we lay stone on stone, that a time is to come when those stones will be held sacred because our hands have touched them, and that men will say, as they look upon the labour and wrought substance of them, "See! This our father did for us."
- John Ruskin

My childhood memories are filled with me wanting to help my father in his fish factory, but he always chased me away and told me to go study. If you read Robert Kiyosaki's book "Rich Dad Poor Dad" you would know what I mean when I say my father was a poor dad. Not poor as a father or financially, but poor in the sense of financial education. I recommend you buy and read this book written by the legend Robert Kiyosaki! In the next few pages I explain the book in detail:

It is the story of a person who has two fathers. The first was his real, biological father, the poor dad and the other one was his best friend, Mikes' dad (a kid of his childhood days who he grew up with) - the rich dad. Both fathers taught Robert how to achieve a level of success but with very different methods and approaches. It becomes evident in the book which fathers approach made more financial sense to Kiyosaki. He compares both fathers to one another.

Their ideas, principles, financial practices and how his real father, the poor and struggling, but highly educated man, was a shadow compared to his rich dad in terms of building assets and general business know how.

His poor dad is compared to those people who are stuck in the Rat Race, those who are trapped in the vicious cycle of needing more but never being able to satisfy their dreams of having more money because of their lack of financial literacy. Learning about money is never taught in school. Instead they teach us about the problems of the world. On the other hand, his rich dad represents the independently wealthy part of society who purposefully takes advantage of the power of corporations and all their personal knowledge of accounting and tax or that of their financial advisers which they manipulate to their advantage.

The theme of the book "Rich Dad Poor Dad" is simple: A can do attitude and fearless entrepreneurship.

These two concepts are highlighted by providing numerous examples for each and focusing on the need for financial literacy, minding your own business, how the power of corporations contribute to making the rich even wealthier, fear, cynicism and other negative attitudes, overcoming obstacles by not promoting laziness, and recognizing the characteristics of human beings and how their preconceived ideas and upbringing affects their financial freedom goals.

There are six major lessons that Robert discusses in the book:

- The rich don't work for money
- The importance of financial literacy
- Minding your own business
- Taxes and corporations
- The rich invent money
- The need to work to learn and not to work for money

The book revolves around three main characters: Poor dad who is Kiyosaki's real father, Rich dad, Kiyosaki's other father and Kiyosaki himself as the son.

The description of each character is:

Poor dad – educated but has no idea of how to be street smart.

Rich dad – has an eighth grade education but is completely street smart

Kiyosaki – the kid who learns lessons from both dads but only adopts the rich dads traits.

The Son (Robert T. Kiyosaki)

I have read this book so many times, I have lost count and every time I read it I learn something new. Robert begins by saying that he is fortunate in having had two fathers.

He learned valuable lessons from both of them, but in Chapter one it becomes clear which father had the more sensible approach towards money.

He compares both dads' views about working hard, getting a solid education, saving and investing and realising how the habits of the rich and poor differ significantly. He attributes his financial knowledge to the many conversations he had with his rich dad.

He stresses the need for accounting knowledge so that the reader clearly understands what assets and liabilities are and takes a common sense approach to the subject of money through simple diagrams that show the inflow and outflow of cash and how the rich build up the asset column and the poor build up the expense column. Robert places much importance on accounting knowledge, no matter how boring the topic is because he says it is "the most important subject in your life".

The rich are the ones who are hardly taxed because they have the knowledge to use tax legislation to their advantage.

Robert also shows his understanding of the tax man and concludes that it is the middle class that actually pay for the poor.

Poor Dad

Kiyosaki compares his poor dad to the millions of fathers out there who encourage their sons to get good grades in school so they can get a good job with a good salary at a corporate company.

Poor dad believed in working hard, saving lots of money the conventional way and not buying material things such as cars and luxury furniture that one cannot afford.

He believed that you should strive to have a good job with a reputable, established company, which Robert already had. That's why he expresses his disappointment when he leaves his job.

Poor dad believes that formal education is the key to success. Although he had a doctorate degree from an Ivy League university he was always financially struggling.

He had the belief that he would never be a really rich man and Robert points out that this became a self fulfilling prophecy.

Poor dad was not interested in the subject of money but more interested in getting a good education.

Roberts' poor dad would always say things like, "money doesn't matter" or "I'm not interested in money".

Poor dad was more worried about the perks of being employed than the job itself. Poor dads' approach to the subject of money was based on working hard to have enough money to pay the bills in contrast to rich dads' approach to make his money work for him.

Rich Dad

Robert realised at nine years old that his rich dad made much more sense than his poor dad. His rich dad taught him not to say, "I can't afford it", but instead to ask the question, "How can I afford it?"

He explains this principle by referring to an incident when he and his best friend, Mike, went to work for Mikes' father.

Rich dad purposefully paid them very little so that it would stir anger and a sense of injustice in them and eventually for them to realise that in order to get ahead, one must work for oneself and not for others.

When Robert complains to rich dad that he can't afford to buy anything with the salary he is paid, rich dad tells him that he shouldn't ponder on the fact that his wages are low, but instead ask, "How can I make more money?", because this stimulates the brain to take action. His rich dad says that when someone says, "I can't afford it", his brain stops working. It therefore kills initiative and promotes being passive and lazy.

Robert says that while his poor dad invested time and effort in education, he did not have any knowledge on investing money.

On the other hand his rich dad was very skilled in the investment game because that's all he did.

The attitude of his rich dad about money is the same as mine as I say it all the time, "The lack of money is the root of all evil". This is in contrast to his poor dads attitude, like many of ours, believing that the love of money is the root of all evil.

Rich dad was the dad who encouraged money talk at the supper table and was portrayed as someone who learned to manage and take calculated risks, instead of not taking risks at all.

Do you see why I say my father was a poor dad; although he was wealthy and always had money he never included us in his business.

He always wanted us to get an education and become part of the corporate world. Well this could be true in the case of one or two of my brothers but I was an entrepreneur.

I remember selling sausage rolls on Saturday mornings at the taxi rank in Paarl. I remember selling fish on the streets at a really early age always wanting to make my own money. My father saw this but always discouraged me, to a point that he would force me to attend varsity so that I wouldn't be able to sell hard.

I attended the prestigious Paarl Boys High School a year before Apartheid ended. If you don't know the history of South Africa, back then you were classed in four race groups: White, Coloured, Indian and Black. My uncle always said that we were unique as we really did not fit into any of these four race groups. In 1992 South Africa was getting ready for its first ever democratic elections.

I remember my first day at Paarl Boys High walking into the best school in the country feeling so lucky and privileged that I was about to start my schooling career at this great school.

What an anti climax! There was this big Afrikaans boy who walked up to me, picked me up and asked me why I looked white and why I had straight hair if I was a "hotnot". How do you answer a question like that?

I looked at him and said that I wasn't and that my forefathers from my dad's side were French and Turkish and that is how they looked. He looked me straight in the eye and head butted me and said that I didn't belong in that school. At thirteen years old this guy changed my perception of Paarl Boys High in one moment and my rebellious days began. The next few months were spent in the principals office as I never felt like I belonged, until one day at the start of rugby season, the astute intervention of a guy who would become one of our countries greatest leaders of men on the rugby field changed my perception towards my beloved Paarl Boys High forever.

Comments by Vefa Enver:

For quite a long time it has been a common tendency for Turkish people to run family businesses. Mostly emotional reasons rather than logical ones lie behind this trend. It is not difficult to see a fathers motive when he desires his offspring to take over the business rather than giving the control of his company to a stranger.

Well I guess that is exactly where most fathers go wrong before one mistake starts leading to another. According to research, with the addition of each new generation in the business, family companies become smaller and smaller.

Just because you are good at what you are doing doesn't mean that your kids will be just as good as you are. From childhood most peoples minds are encoded with the idea that when the time comes they will continue what their father started and take it much further. A job taken for granted! Why would any one take any challenge in life if they already know what the future holds for them?

Underpriviliged people, knowing that they have to start from scratch, work twice or even three times harder than a privileged person. Maybe that is why they become the most inspiring success stories.

You never know how strong you are until being strong becomes your only option.

The worst thing you can do to your children is give them everything that they want and leave them without any dreams or wishes to come true. It is almost like domesticating an animal then expecting him to survive in the wild. Let's face it, no matter how much we try to protect our kids, it is inevitable that they will eventually learn that it is a wild world waiting out there.

We must encourage our kids to find their potentials through both academic and practical life.

When the time comes we must let them fly away from home and have their own life experiences and make their own mistakes.

If they find a better place which suits them more, then that is where they will be happy and successful. If they fly back home, at least they will know for sure it is where they belong.

What Vefa doesn't realise is that I wanted that! What she is saying is not

34

true for all children. We as parents need to see which child should be guided into entrepreneurship and which should go and study.

I wanted to run the family business, I wanted to carry on with the legacy! I ended up doing it anyway. (More on that later).

Chapter 3: Impact of good leaders

"Management is doing things right; leadership is doing the right things."

Peter Drucker

Corné Krige was my senior... an eighteen year old matric boy whose name was always half whispered when uttered, like he was some sort of god or ghost. His legend and myth was widespread amongst us juniors. South Africa is a rugby mad country and Paarl Boys High ranks among the top five rugby playing schools of all time.

Corné Krige was our first team captain, Western Province under 19 player and later that year, South African schools captain.

He would go on to lead our country and was arguably the toughest Springbok of his generation. I had the privilege of experiencing his leadership qualities and natural sales skills at an early age.

I was a rebel in grade 8. At thirteen years old, the system in 1993 did not work for me. I was always made to feel like an outsider, but the astute intervention of a true leader slowly converted me and made me feel part of it all.

My first experience with Corné came after school one afternoon when our first side was about to travel by bus to play a night game in Worcester in Boland. The announcement was made during break that a bus would be leaving at 4pm to take anyone who wants to go watch the game to the stadium on a first come first served basis as there were limited seats.

I made sure that I was there at 2pm and waited for two hours to book my seat on the bus. I saw Corné smiling and watching me from his hostel balcony. I was in awe of the guy so I just looked away out of fear and respect.

When the bus arrived it filled up quickly. I was first to get my seat. As the senior boys arrived, the head coach made an announcement that the bus was too full and pointed to me and said that I should leave. I was devastated! I stood up and almost in tears made my way to the front.

It is at that moment that I had my first experience of a great leader. Corné stood up, and in a confident, almost arrogant tone said in Afrikaans: "Coach he was here first, he can have my seat, I will stand". That gesture made everyone in the bus look at me and at that moment, the feelings toward me changed.

It was as if Corné gave me his personal endorsement. He signalled to me to move to the back and I sat next to him. The entire bus drive he showed an interest in who I was and assured me that I will do well in this school. That year, every time he would walk past me he would just smirk as Corné does, and say a simple "howzit" with some sort of look as if to say, "are you ok, you still hanging in there?"

His acknowledgement made my peers accept me even more as the "famous" Corné Krige actually knew who I was.

Later on in his career, the media criticised him a lot for his never say die attitude on the rugby field.

I always supported him and indirectly, he played a big part in me being so involved in my beloved Alma Mater Paarl Boys High. Corné, I salute you.

My second glimpse of a true leader came in the form of a guy called Richard Visagie.

My final year at high school saw me being the most popular guy in school. I was captain of the A team hockey every year at every age group level, a model student and head of the "Gees Komitee". This is a group of leaders who did not make the cut to be prefects but had the qualities to lead the school.

I was honoured and took my task really seriously.   Mr Visagie placed me on the committee and told me that everyone in this school followed me and that I could probably be one of the best old boys this school has ever produced. Every time there was a problem in the school regarding pupils he would publically say to me: "Moerat, you know your role" so as to endorse me as a leader. He was a great mentor and I have the utmost respect for him.

Even though my school years were memorable and I had the privilege to be prepped by great leaders, my final year proved to be my biggest life test to date.

At seventeen, life threw me the biggest curveball. My father slowly started losing everything. The next two years were spent wandering, surviving, navigating and just trying to make ends meet. Later on in life I would describe those years as the best thing that could ever have happened to me. Those were indirectly the best years of my life.

It's different when you grow up poor because you don't know anything else and all of a sudden having nothing at the stage in your life when you needed everything was the best life lesson anyone could get. As the months went by we started losing cars, furniture and all the material things. We as brothers actually became closer, but that was the year my parents got divorced. My father always wanted us close to him. Even though he couldn't afford to and he was going through tough times, he always made sure that we were ok, even if it was just in the form of a phone call or a kind word.

I was ok with losing my car, my nice clothes and all the material things, but when you lose your home that you were born in and had grown up in... I wouldn't wish that upon anyone.

A lot of my family might hate me for saying this but I feel that the little mercy that was shown towards my father and his sons, especially me, made me who I am today. That's why I show so much mercy towards others and help wherever I can.

Yes, I was an arrogant, spoilt young boy but I was always a fighter which my dad was not and he needed me to portray the role of the bad guy. I don't regret doing that. I want to take this opportunity to thank them for playing such a big role in my way of thinking today. I can honestly say with the exception of a few, no one was there for me and that is why today I am there for others.

The final night at our house was the cherry on top. I remember my dad being so nervous and stressed all week. He called us into the living room and said that it would be the last night that we would be together in that house. I think that was the most difficult thing my dad ever had to do. At that moment a leader was born. When my dad eventually left the room I looked at my brothers and told them that we are not destined for this. It was only a phase, it was not written in our stars. We were meant to be leaders and we were meant to be wealthy. This was not our fate. I told them to go out there and learn as much as possible as one day we would do it for ourselves. In the years that followed each one of them ended up working for good companies, taking in as much as they could. Today I am proud to say we are doing it for ourselves... as partners.

Ten years later I bought back the house we lost, the business we lost, the cars we lost and made it bigger and better than my father could ever dream of. More on that in my third book titled "Good Enough Doesn't Cut It".

At this point, after discussing my first two leaders,   I would like to discuss six different leadership styles and when you should use them.

Taking any team from under-achieving to excelling means understanding and embracing the difference between management and leadership. Whether it is in sports or business, the same fundamental principles exist.

"Management is doing things right; leadership is doing the right things."

I firmly believe that any sales team or organisation is only as strong as its leader. In my sales career I have worked under many managers, community and sports club leaders. Most were poor, few were great.

'Manager' and 'leader' are two completely different roles, although people often use the terms interchangeably. Managers are facilitators of their team members' successes.

A manager ensures that his team has everything they need to produce results and be successful. He ensures that they are well-trained and have sufficient product knowledge or know the game plan.

He makes sure that they are happy and have very few stumbling blocks in their path and that they are being groomed to take it to the next level.

He also gives recognition for great performance and coaches his troops through their obstacles and challenges.

For the purpose of not naming and shaming my subjects, I will refer to this leader as 'Mr Potato Head'.

I worked under Mr Potato Head for three years. This guy was clueless and did not have any knowledge of the department he was running. I ended up doing all the work as his second in charge and the team saw this.

He had no credibility and when the company retrenched, he was first to go.

He did everything wrong that a manager possibly could and thought he was doing the opposite by letting me run the team. I wish Mr Potato head all the best. He was a good guy, but a bad manager.

A leader however can be anyone in the company or on the team who has a certain talent, who is forward thinking and creatively thinks out of the box and has great ideas, who has the most experience in a certain part of the business or project that can be useful to the manager and the team.

A leader leads based on ability, example and strengths, not titles. That is what I was to Mr Potato Head. The leader of the team. No title, just leading by example and knowledge.

The best managers are always allowing different leaders to emerge and stand up and be counted on to inspire their teammates and themselves to reach the next level.

When you're dealing with ongoing business and life challenges and constant changes, and you're in unfamiliar territory not knowing what comes next, no one can expect you to have all the answers or rule the team with an iron fist based solely on the title you hold.

Most of the times you will need the collective support of the leaders in your team to see you through those tough tasks. The best leaders don't just create followers they create more leaders within their team. At my companies, when my brothers and I share leadership, we're all a lot smarter, more flexible and more capable in running the companies, especially when that road is so full of unknown and unforeseen challenges.

The greatest teammates not only allow different leaders to consistently emerge based on their strengths, but also they realise that leadership should be situational, depending on the needs of the team. Sometimes a colleague or team mate needs a high five.

Sometimes the team needs a go getter, a forward thinker, a visionary, perhaps a new style of coaching maybe, someone to lead the way or even, on occasion, someone to light a fire under their butts!

Great leaders choose their leadership style like a fly half in rugby chooses his boots, with a careful analysis of the task at hand, the end goal and the best tool to get the ball through the poles.

In a landmark 2000 Harvard Business Review study on the subject of kinetic leadership, Daniel Golemans' "Leadership That Gets Results" found that a managers' leadership style was responsible for 30% of the companies' profitability! That's way too much to ignore.

43

Their aim was to uncover specific leadership behaviours and determine their effect on the corporate climate and each leadership styles' effect on profitability.

Here are the six leadership styles they uncovered among the managers that were studied:

1. The pacesetting leader "Do as I do, now".

2. The authoritative leader "Come with me".

3. The affiliative leader "People come first".

4. The coaching leader "Try this".

5. The coercive leader "Do what I tell you".

6. The democratic leader "What do you think?"

There is no perfect leadership style. It is all situational and a good leader knows when to use which style. In my life I was fortunate enough to always lead.

From a very young age it became evident that I was born to lead when others would only follow. I've always tried to lead by example and to make decisions based on my experiences and although I don't always get it right, I am always learning from it. The best advice I can give you is that if you take a cup of authoritative leadership, a cup of democratic, coaching, and affiliative leadership, and a little bit of pacesetting and coercive leadership and you lead in a way that lifts and inspires your team, you have an excellent recipe for long term leadership success with every team or organisation you will ever lead in your life.

Top 10 Qualities That Make a Great Leader

An article featured on www.forbes.com by Tanya Prive:

Having a great, bright idea, and assembling a strong team to bring that concept to life is the first step in creating a successful long lasting business venture.

While finding a new and unique idea is so rare; the ability to successfully execute this idea is what separates the dreamers from the entrepreneurs.

No matter how you see yourself, as soon as you make that exciting first hire, you have taken the first steps in becoming a powerful leader.

The stress levels are high when money is tight and the visions of instant success don't happen like you thought, it's easy to let those emotions get to you when you are not making the money you thought you would and this will affect your team.

Remind yourself of the leader you are and would like to become.

Here are some key qualities that every good leader should possess, and learn to emphasize.

Honesty

Whatever ethics you believe in and hold yourself to, when you are responsible for a team of people, it's important to raise the bar even higher.

Your business and its employees are a reflection of yourself, and if you make honest and ethical behaviour a key value, your team will follow suit.

Try to make a list of values and core beliefs that both you and your brand represent, and post this in your office. Promote a healthy inter-office lifestyle, and encourage your team to live up to these standards.

By emphasising these standards, and displaying them yourself, you will hopefully influence the office environment to be a friendly and helpful workspace.

Ability to Delegate

Finessing your brand vision is essential to creating an organized and efficient business, but if you don't learn to trust your team with that vision, you might never progress to the next stage.

It's important to remember that trusting your team with your idea is a sign of strength, not weakness. Delegating tasks to the appropriate departments is one of the most important skills you can develop as your business grows. The emails and tasks will begin to pile up, and the more you stretch yourself thin, the lower the quality of your work will become, and the less you will produce.

The key to delegation is identifying the strengths of your team, and capitalizing on them. Find out what each team member enjoys doing most. Chances are if they find that task more enjoyable, they will likely put more thought and effort behind it.

This will not only prove to your team that you trust and believe in them, but will also free up your time to focus on the higher level tasks, that should not be delegated. It's a fine balance, but one that will have a huge impact on the productivity of your business.

Communication

Knowing what you want accomplished may seem clear in your head, but if you try to explain it to someone else and are met with a blank expression, you know there is a problem. If this has been your experience, then you may want to focus on honing your communication skills.

Being able to clearly and succinctly describe what you want done is extremely important. If you can't relate your vision to your team, you won't all be working towards the same goal.

Training new members and creating a productive work environment all depend on healthy lines of communication. Whether that stems from an open-door policy to your office, or making it a point to talk to your staff on a daily basis, making yourself available to discuss inter-office issues is vital. Your team will learn to trust and depend on you, and will be less hesitant to work harder.

Sense of Humour

If your website crashes, you lose that major client, or your funding dries up, guiding your team through the process without panicking is as challenging as it is important.

Morale is linked to productivity, and it's your job as the team leader to instil a positive energy. That's where your sense of humour will finally pay off. Encourage your team to laugh at the mistakes instead of crying. If you are constantly learning to find the humour in the struggles, your work environment will become a happy and healthy space, one which your employees look forward to working in, rather than dreading it.

Make it a point to crack jokes with your team and encourage personal discussions of weekend plans and trips. It's these short breaks from the task at hand that help keep productivity levels high and morale even higher.

Confidence

There may be days where the future of your brand is worrisome and things aren't going according to plan.

This is true with any business, large or small, and the most important thing is not to panic. Part of your job as a leader is to put out fires and maintain the team morale.

Keep up your confidence level, and assure everyone that setbacks are natural and the important thing is to focus on the larger goal.

As the leader, by staying calm and confident, you will help keep the team feeling the same. Remember, your team will take cues from you, so if you exude a level of calm damage control, your team will pick up on that feeling. The key objective is to keep everyone working and moving ahead.

Commitment

If you expect your team to work hard and produce quality content, you're going to need to lead by example. There is no greater motivation than seeing the boss down in the trenches working alongside everyone else, showing that hard work is being done on every level.

By proving your commitment to the brand and your role, you will not only earn the respect of your team, but will also instil that same hardworking energy among your staff.

It's important to show your commitment not only to the work at hand, but also to your promises. If you pledged to host a holiday party, or uphold summer Fridays, keep your word. You want to create a reputation for not just working hard, but also too be known as a fair leader. Once you have gained the respect of your team, they are more likely to deliver the peak amount of quality work possible.

Positive Attitude

You want to keep your team motivated towards the continued success of the company, and keep the energy levels up. Whether that means providing snacks, coffee, relationship advice, or even just an occasional beer in the office, remember that everyone on your team is a person. Keep the office mood a fine balance between productivity and playfulness.

If your team is feeling happy and upbeat, chances are they won't mind staying that extra hour to finish a report, or devoting their best work to the brand.

Creativity

Some decisions will not always be so clear-cut. You may be forced at times to deviate from your set course and make an on the fly decision. This is where your creativity will prove to be vital. It is during these critical situations that your team will look to you for guidance and you may be forced to make a quick decision.

As a leader, it's important to learn to think outside the box and to choose which of two bad choices is the best option. Don't immediately choose the first or easiest possibility; sometimes it is best to give these issues some thought, and even turn to your team for guidance. By utilizing all possible options before making a rash decision, you can typically reach the end conclusion you were aiming for.

Intuition

When leading a team through uncharted waters, there is no roadmap on what to do. Everything is uncertain, and the higher the risk, the higher the pressure. That is where your natural intuition has to kick in.

Guiding your team through the process of your day-to-day tasks can be honed down to a science.

But when something unexpected occurs, or you are thrown into a new scenario, your team will look to you for guidance.

Drawing on past experience is a good reflex, as is reaching out to your mentors for support.

Eventually though, the tough decisions will be up to you to decide and you will need to depend on your gut instinct for answers.

Learning to trust yourself is as important as your team learning to trust you.

Ability to Inspire

Creating a business often involves a bit of forecasting. Especially in the beginning stages of a start up, inspiring your team to see the vision of the successes to come is vital.

Make your team feel invested in the accomplishments of the company.

Whether everyone owns a piece of equity, or you operate on a bonus system, generating enthusiasm for the hard work you are all putting in is so important.

Being able to inspire your team is great for focusing on the future goals, but it is also important for the current issues.

When you are all mired deep in work, morale is low, and energy levels are fading, recognize that everyone needs a break now and then.

Acknowledge the work that everyone has dedicated and commend the team on each of their efforts. It is your job to keep spirits up, and that begins with an appreciation for the hard work.

"Credited to Tanya Prive"

Comments by Vefa Enver:

"What doesn't kill you makes you stronger."

There is a life experience behind every saying and we never realise it until the same reality hits us. Good times make good memories but hard times make good life lessons.

Leaders are never born under favourable circumstances. Not everyone is born to be a leader but at least everyone can lead their own life, if they choose to be behind the steering wheel, in total control. To be able to grow into our full personality we need to go through difficulties.

I know we would all rather take the "milky way" and constantly rise but unfortunately things do not work that way and sometimes it is inevitable to fall. There are two kinds of approaches towards life when you feel like you are thrown to the ground: You either get up, dust yourself off and get going or keep lying down on the floor feeling pity for yourself. It is ok to feel devastated at the first hit of the storm.

There's nothing more human than feeling lost, angry and even totally hopeless when things quickly turn upside down in an unexpected way.

Somehow after the rage subsides it is confidence in ourselves that will determine our way of acting. A relative of mine who is quite old now once said: "There is no goal I can't reach once I put my mind to it.

I might rise, I might fall, I might lose it all and then get it all back." And I grew up watching this man making a great fortune and then losing it for he liked to take big risks.

In a few years he would start rising up again to lose some of it with another risk he was willing to take.

What I learned from him is that life is like riding on a roller coaster. Only the ones who clasp the thrill without fear and take in each moment they live fully enjoy the ride.

But then again those ones turn every opportunity into success. After all life is a big game called Truth or Dare. Some of us are busy finding the TRUTH while the rest DARE make their dreams come true.

Chapter 4: Objection handling

"You may not control all the events that happen to you, but you can decide not to be reduced by them."

Maya Angelou

I remember that day clearly. The day I walked into ForwardSlash offices... again, with my CV in my hand.

I seem to do that often. Just walk into a company and sell myself. An opportunity arose in the call centre at this international online gaming company as an inbound entertainment executive dealing with customer queries worldwide.

After two months in the call centre, I took the initiative to start prospecting and calling clients to get them spending more. As the company had no outbound department, I was the only one doing so. I saw the need for an entire department and "pitched" the call centre head to let me recruit a team and start a department from scratch.

He gave me one month to prove to him why. That month I met and exceeded all sales and inventory targets and my request was granted.

One month later, I had a team of 12-14 agents running 24/7, calling the world and converting players at a rate of 14 per agent per shift.

I quickly developed a reputation as Mr Sales, often working 18 hour shifts, 7 days a week.

During this period, I compiled, formatted and edited the training manual (Telemarketing the Entertainer's Approach). A training manual based on selling telephonically in an entertaining manner.

I made my move to online media when the media buyers were struggling to close deals. It was the next logical step as media buying was all about negotiating deals, "negotiating", the brother of "selling". I spent four years at ForwardSlash.

This chapter will be dedicated to objection handling; the body of all sales and negotiations. As in life, as in sales there are always objections. It is a natural process. You will always have to overcome them.

Sales people spend a lot of time and effort to find prospects that they can sell their product or services to.

Yet, no matter how certain the need or precise the market definition, prospects will always have questions and objections, concerns, and requests for more information.

You should welcome these objections because once you have answered them correctly they give you the potential energy to close the deal fast and effectively.

In the sales industry, one definition of an objection is "any reason given by the prospective customer why they are not ready to buy into your product or service".

Objections are obstacles that need to be overcome.

Every objection can be answered. Many people will make use of objections to avoid making decisions or commitments and not necessarily because they don't want to buy from you.

However, you might be facing your most difficult close when your prospect doesn't have any objections!

Your success as a salesman will depend on your ability to anticipate and handle a prospects' objection smoothly.

No matter how solid or thorough you think your sale pitch or presentation is, at some point, the prospect will throw an objection at you, and how you handle it will make the difference on whether you close effectively or not.

New salesmen dread objections! It is natural because they are not sure they can find convincing arguments to counter them.

However, veteran salesmen have learned how to take the prospects' objection and turn it around in order to close effectively.

Before you make your presentation review it in detail. Every time you get to a point where you think there might be an objection, write it down and give it to a friend and ask him or her to give you any objections that come to mind.

Practise your answers while role playing. You may not be able to come up with all of the answers to make your presentation "objection proof", but you will surely have control of the sale pitch and be equipped with lots of possible answers in the event that questions do come up.

The ability to anticipate objections is very important, but not nearly as important as the skills you need to develop that will be necessary to overcome your prospects' valid concerns about your product or service.

By always using a client-centred approach where you provide all of the facts necessary, it will work well in overcoming any objection. When you welcome objections and not ignore them, you are communicating to the prospect that his needs are important and will be addressed.

Examples of this approach would be:

"I understand what you are saying and I agree with you. Another person asked the same questions. Here's how I worked with him to satisfy his concerns…"

Or

"If we could make sure the payment plan will meet your requirements, would there still be a problem?"

Or

"I'm glad you mentioned that because it gives me the chance to show you how this product will improve your life and make it more enjoyable."

Honesty and integrity coupled with skill will take you far in your presentation. Don't ever tell the prospect what you think they want to hear. Today's people are better prepared and more practical than in the past.

If you listen to the prospect and acknowledge his objections as being valid, answer them truthfully and satisfy their need, you will be offering so much more additional justification for the prospect to buy into what you are selling.

Objections are NOT the boogy man! Expect them and allow the person to express them freely and answer him.

Welcome the questions when they occur because they indicate an interest on the part of the prospect. If he has no questions or objections, start worrying because he is not buying!

Give complete answers to the objections. Draw upon any testimonials, experiences from the past or whatever relevant information you have at hand.

A good way of buying time to think is to affirm the objection by restating it in the form of a question to be answered.

"So what you are saying is that the price concerns you, isn't it?"

Or you can stall and not respond immediately. He will most definitely continue talking to clarify his position or to give you more information. When this happens, wait a couple of seconds and think about what he has just said. Your pause will show a level of respect and he will know that you are listening to what he has just said.

Objections are just requests for more information! If you look at objections as just this and nothing more, you will see that you end up answering all of them with confidence. Look at objections as being a prospects' request for more information about your product or service and nothing else. If you want to close, you must give them the information they are looking for. Do this and your discussions will move smoothly and you'll move closer to a positive decision. If the prospect seems to be stalling after you answered all of his objections, the reason might be one of these:

He's not completely sold on your product or service, he wants to get other proposals from other companies or he is not the decision maker!

 Ask probing questions to determine what his problem is. "Are you not sure about our payment methods?" "What is holding you back in making your decision?" "Are you not thinking of adding the life cover to your existing benefits?"

If he is not the decision maker, then get the decision maker on the line!

Some of the more common objections and how to handle them:

"Your asking price is way too much."

This is by far the most common objection out there and perhaps the most difficult one to handle. Often prices, for the most part, are "cast in concrete", and not easily changed. You must present a benefit oriented solution to the objection by quantifying your product by building value. My second book, "The Next Best Thing" covers the sales process namely: Qualify - Quantify - Close

"I can get it cheaper somewhere else."

Two good answers to this objection are: "No problem sir, I understand what you are saying. But let me ask you this... have you ever chosen the lowest price in the past and have been disappointed?" Or, "Is your primary goal 'price' or are you also interested in service delivery, quality, reliability and years in the industry?"

"I don't have the time to discuss that right now."

Respond with: "If you don't like what I am about to say feel free to walk away or drop the phone in my ear at any time".

"Why haven't I heard about your company before?"

A good answer is, "We tend to spend less on advertising and more on giving our clients the attention they deserve through customer benefits like our Rewards Program".

"I have to speak to my wife."

I am not going to answer this one for you! Go and see Boiler Room, the movie I discuss in chapter nine and you will learn first hand how to answer this common objection.

"How long has your company been in business?"

You might want to ask the prospect: "I know you have been with us for a long time. I am willing to bet that you have seen many people who have been around for quite a while that will not give you the kind of service we will!" Or, "Yes, we are a young business with a limited client base, but you can be sure we treat our clients as people who are very, very important."

In closing, one fact that you will have to make peace with is that as a salesperson, you will not close every deal.

Some will fall away, no, most will fall away. You have no real control over that.

However, you can avoid those situations by preparing yourself well in advance; have a great sales pitch that you know off by heart.

Ensure that you practise it in front of your colleagues and be sure to identify all the objections within your proposal and have answers to them. Then, go out there and give it your best. You will win some and you will lose some. It is part of this game we love!

"Some will like you; some won't like you; so what?"

You know what, "NO" just gets me started anyways...

Jamie knows I love a nice nargila and she can make the best pipes. Nothing close to what I get in Istanbul but hey, beggars can't be choosers right?

She also has a few "NO's" that I've learned to work with. If I ask her to make me a pipe and she says, 'not now', I just get out the tobacco and coals and promise to smoke outside and in five minutes I have my nargila. This is her first "NO" and as you can see, it is easily overcome.

Her second "NO" is a little more difficult. It is usually stated strongly but I can overcome it easily with something like, "I'll get the pipe out and assemble it and have the fruit ready as soon as you light the coals, OK?"

This usually works. Her third "NO" is more difficult to overcome. It is usually very firm and followed by something like, "I don't have time so DON'T BOTHER ME WITH IT!" I usually just change the subject for a moment and go about getting out the pipe and coals and tobacco and end up helping her.

Lesson learnt:

"No's" are really just buying signals and the start of the sales process. A "No" usually means a lack of information on how the product or service can benefit a prospect. So from now on, treat "No's" as an opportunity not rejection!

Rejection and sales go hand in hand. You have to get use to people telling you "No" all the time. Especially with telemarketing as it follows the law of large numbers. This means that the more calls you make, the higher the probability of success.

Example: Out of one thousand calls, you'll get hold of two hundred people to pitch to and close twenty of them.

It also means that one hundred and eighty people would have said "No"! This is just the nature of the game.

Never take these "NO's" personally.

You have to get through a certain number of "No's" before you can get to a "Yes". In fact, every time you hear someone say "No" you should be so happy because you're that much closer to getting your next "Yes"!

Imagine how boring the job would be if everyone you pitched said yes on every single call!

Where's the challenge? I'd be bored in no time! So just consider rejection as a part of the game.

Objections stay objections, irrespective of which industry you are in. Whether you are selling cars, insurance or hawking on the streets, in a call centre, face to face or even via email. There will always be objections in life and sales. I said it before; I will say it again... Welcome them!

Comments by Vefa Enver:

"I saw the need for an entire department and "pitched" the call centre head to let me recruit a team and start a department from scratch. He gave me one month to prove to him why. That month I met and exceeded all sales and inventory targets and my request was granted. One month later I had a team of 12-14 agents running 24/7, calling the world and converting players at a rate of 14 per agent per shift. I quickly developed a reputation as Mr Sales, often working 18 hour shifts 7 days a week.

This very part reminds me of George Bernard Shaw's words:

"Life isn't about finding yourself. Life is about creating yourself."

People mostly complain about what they lack in their lives: luck, opportunity, circumstances, fairness. On the other hand they are rarely thankful for what they have already got. People have the tendancy to be blind to their own assets because of focusing too much on others.

For everything they don't have they blame the injustice of life but it takes wisdom to realise that until they believe in themselves they do not truly believe in God. Don't get me wrong. By no means do I suggest losing your ambition to achieve more in life by simply being happy and content with what you already have but it helps a lot when thinking and feeling that all the necessary tools you need are already provided when you come into this world.

Chapter 5: It's not what you say but how you say it

"All the great speakers were bad speakers at first."

Ralph Waldo Emerson

You know that in your job as a salesman you will need to master the art of persuasive communication to get people to buy into what you are saying and take action on only the words coming from your mouth. Like I said earlier, entertain him into making a decision. There is no substitute for the proper use of positive phrases coupled with good movement. Remember, motion creates emotion.

Persuasive communication does not mean overwhelming the person with an overload of all the important sounding words in your vocabulary, or making unrealistic claims and promises that you won't be able to keep. It simply means being a really effective and clear communicator, who is energetic and always enthusiastic about the message he is bringing across, sounds interested in meeting and exceeding the needs of the prospect, and can make any person trust him, in matter of minutes, using only his words and body language.

One of my favourite tools when pitching or being interviewed is the use of transitions. Transitions are phrases that do three things simultaneously. It controls the conversation, acknowledges that you heard the prospect and you're now going to respond and it buys you the time to find the correct response without stuttering like an idiot.

Transitions are just simple phrases that contain no product knowledge at all. It allows you to get back into the conversation or sales pitch and buys you time to think about the proper responses without wasting time or having those uncomfortable pauses.

Examples of transitions are:

I definitely hear what you're saying and…

Ok, I can appreciate that and…

You know, I completely understand and...

Well, I see what you mean and…

Notice the word, 'and' at the end of all of these examples. The word, 'and' is smooth, unassertive, and non confrontational.

Whenever I am really stuck while being interviewed or while presenting and I can't find the right response or the correct word, I'll just roll some of these together!

I was interviewed for the Mr South Africa competition in 2013 which I judged, and I was interrupted with a question that threw me off guard because it was really controversial. Instead of sounding like a complete idiot by stuttering, pausing and acting like a monkey, I bought time to structure my response with: "You know what, that's a very good question... very good question indeed.

I'd like to mention that I hear what you're saying and I see what you mean and I'd like to reassure you that..." Now I bought about ten seconds to think before I answer.

The absolute best transition is the 'paraphrase'. Just repeat and clarify what the person said to you so you can buy a little time to get to the right response.

Prospect: What do I need to qualify for this? Are there any requirements from my side?

Paraphrase: A lot of people that I call ask what the qualifying requirements are and let me explain to you that...

I once called a difficult client who said: "I only take telesales calls on Sunday nights when cows are jumping over the moon".

My answer was: "That's great! Because I'm calling you from a farm in Paarl with a lot of cows and I just noticed the full moon last night and..."

I followed with a benefit.

Naturally he laughed and that broke the ice and he ended up buying from me.

Little "Yeses" add up to that big "YES"!

A good sales script should take away or answer objections before they're asked and when done properly, you need to get him to say "Yes" a few times.

The verification of a prospects details is the perfect way to get him to say "Yes" a few times. Making your prospect say "yes" all the time is the ultimate psychology of sales.

Consider this sale scenario where the salesman knows all the prospects details.

Agent: And your first name is Paul?

Prospect: Yes

Agent: And your last name is Johnson?

Prospect: Yes

Agent: And your street address is 1 Hope Street?

Prospect: Yes

Agent: And your city is Wellington?

Prospect: Yes

Agent: And your province is Western Cape and your phone number is 555-1234678?

Prospect: Yes

Agent: And you want me to sign you up, right?

Prospect: Yes!

See how much easier it is?

Features and Benefits

In my second book titled "The Next Best Thing" I take you through the entire sales process and my ultimate favourite technique namely:

"Feature-Benefit-Closing Question"

I will touch on explaining the difference between a feature and a benefit but you will need to read book two to understand the full use of the technique mentioned above.

Knowing the advantages and benefits of your product is of utmost importance. It is your key selling point!

Always list the benefits and advantages of using the product you are selling. Never list the disadvantages unless the prospect asks a direct question. Do not list more negative points if you are not asked directly!

Remember that customers do not buy products; they buy what products do for them.

A feature is a fact. It is part of the build of the product.

A benefit is the personal advantage of the product features.

Products should be described in terms of their features and benefits.

Features are product characteristics such as height, size, colour, horsepower, functionality, design, hours of business, fabric content, material, etc.

Benefits are simple. It answers the customers' question: What's in it for me?

A feature is physical size: "It is small enough to fit in your back pocket".

A benefit is: "You will not have to carry it in a bag".

A feature is: "As part of our service we negotiate discounts for you".

A benefit is: "You will save money all the time".

Positive Language

Language is one of the most powerful tools a salesman can possess.

Whether you communicate orally, or in writing, the way you express yourself, the way you sound and project your voice and the way you move while speaking will affect whether your message is received positively or negatively.

Even when you are conveying unpleasant and negative news, the impact on your listeners can be softened by the use of what we call positive language.

Negative and Positive Language

Negative language often tells the listener what cannot be done and has a subtle tone of blame. Simple!

It is words like can't, won't, unable to, that tell the listener everything that you can't do.

It does not promote positive action or positive consequences.

Positive phrasing and language sounds helpful and encouraging rather than discouraging.

It tells the listener what can be done and suggests alternatives and choices available to the prospect or audience.

It stresses positive actions and positive consequences.

Common use of Negative Language

Expressions that suggest carelessness:

You neglected to specify...

You failed to include...

You overlooked enclosing...

TRY: If you can send us (whatever), we can complete the process for you.

Phrases that suggest the person is lying:

You claim that...

You say that...

You state that...

TRY: The information we have suggests that you have a different viewpoint on this issue. Allow me to explain our perspective.

Expressions that imply that the prospect is a monkey:

We cannot see how you...

We fail to understand...

We are at a loss to know...

TRY: Might we suggest that you...

Demanding phrases that imply pressure:

You should...

You ought to...

You must...

We must ask you to...

We must insist...

TRY: One option open to you is.

Phrases that might be interpreted as sarcastic or patronising:

No doubt...

We will thank you to...

You understand, of course...

Please respond soon...

TRY: We can help you to (whatever) if you can send us (whatever)

A few suggestions on where to start:

You will be pleased to know...

We are pleased to inform you...

Kindly note...

Please be aware...

Please be advised...

We would like to take this opportunity...

Please be reminded...

We are pleased to confirm...

I love this inspirational Story on the use of positive language:

A Middle Eastern king had a dream. He dreamt that all his teeth fell out, one after the other. Very upset about this, he summoned his dream interpreter.

The man listened with great concern to the kings' account of his dream and said to him: "Your majesty, I have bad news for you. Just as you lost all your teeth, you will lose all of your family, one after another".

This sad interpretation aroused the kings' rage.   The dream interpreter, who had nothing better to offer, was thrown into jail at the kings' command.

He summoned a different dream interpreter. The second man heard him tell his dream and said: "Your majesty, I have good news for you. You will reach a greater age than any member of your family.

You will outlive them all." The king rejoiced and rewarded the man richly for this.

But the courtiers were very surprised. "Your words were really no different from your poor predecessor's. Why was he punished while you received a reward?" they asked.

The second dream interpreter replied:

"You are right; we both interpreted the dream in the same way.

But the important thing is not only what you say, but how you say it."

Call with news they'll have an interest in or ideas you've heard from other customers they might be able to take advantage of. Mention that you were "thinking of them" and tell them why.

Example:

"The promotional department called to say that they just launched a new promotion and wanted you to be the first to know, and thought you could benefit from it." It's little things like that, which cause clients to say: "They always have something good for me when they call", as opposed to, "Every time they call they are just looking for money".

Comments by Vefa Enver:

It is with words through which we communicate our thoughts to another person. Negative words can have long lasting results far more than we might anticipate. Although body language too has an important place in interaction with people, verbal expression is the main and the most important tool.

Just as Johann Wolfgang von Goethe said: "if you wish to know the mind of a man, listen to his words."

Words have great impact on people yet we mostly fail to stop and think of the consequences before we speak. In return what we get is mostly the subconscious reaction of the other persons brain. Like in the example given below.

The word, 'and' is smooth, unassertive, and not confrontational.

When the word, 'but' is used at the end of a transitional phrase, I just visualise the person bracing for the attack of fine print that's sure to follow.

Why do we get a negative signal from our brains when we hear the word "but" and not "and"?

Because our brains disregard the sentence which comes before "but" once our ears hear that word.

When you say "I really liked your drawing but it would be better if you used more pale colours".

My brain will ignore the first part of the sentence and I will get the feeling:

"I didn't like your drawing because I think the colours are too bright."

Whether intentionally or unintentionally we leave impression on people with every word we choose. It is our own initiative to be constructive or destructive by uttering "fruitful" or "hurtful" words.

The characteristics of fruitful words are:

Constructive: They help to build good communication among people. Utterance of each well chosen word accompanied by a warm and friendly attitude is like laying bricks of a solid building one by one.

Timely: Like in every other aspect of life, timing is also very important here. The right words at the wrong time can be just as damaging as the wrong words.

It's required to know when and if you should speak. Words left unsaid can also be hurtful.

Graceful: A person can have two kinds of impression on people with his/her choice of words: Either make them want to put more effort into the job by empowering them or make them want to give up by diminishing them.

Chapter 6: Top Sales movies ever! PG 18

"There's no such thing as too far. You understand? You push everything as far as you can. You push and you push and you push until it starts pushing back. And then you push some goddamn more."

Walter Abrams - Two for the Money

I am a sucker for a good sales movie and have seen all the greats a hundred times! From "Thank you for smoking" to "The Pursuit of Happiness", from "Jerry McGuire" to "Cadillac Man" to "Two for the Money".

I must admit that the Wall Street movies with Michael Douglas are right up there but there are two movies that taught me so much about selling I felt it necessary to go into detail and explain why these movies had such an impact on my career. This chapter has a PG 18 rating!

1. Glengarry Glen Ross

Times are tough in a Chicago real estate office. The salesmen (Shelley Levene, Ricky Roma, Dave Moss, and George Aaronow) are given a huge incentive by Blake to succeed in a sales contest. First prize is a Cadillac Eldorado, second prize is a set of steak knives and third prize is "You're fired!" There is no room for losers in this dramatically masculine world of sales; only "closers" will get the good sales leads, the Glengarry leads.

There is a lot of pressure on the guys to succeed, so a robbery is committed which has unforeseen consequences for all the characters.

The following scene by Alec Baldwin is one of the best scenes by a sales manager EVER in a movie.

I know it off by heart and have seen this movie over a hundred times. I suggest you do the same!

Blake: Let me have your attention for a moment! Cause you're talking about what? You're talking about... *[Puts out his cigarette]* ...bitching about that sale you shot, some son of a b.... don't want to buy land, somebody don't want what you're selling, some broad you're trying to screw, so forth. Let's talk about something important. *[To John Williamson]* Are they all here?

John Williamson: All but one.

Blake: Well, I'm going anyway. Let's talk about something important! *[To Shelley "The Machine" Levene]* Put that coffee down!! Coffee's for closers only. *[Shelley scoffs]* You think I'm f....ng with you? I am not f....ng with you. I'm here from downtown. I'm here for Mitch and Murray. And I'm here on a mission of mercy. Your name's Levene?

Shelley "The Machine" Levene: Yeah.

Blake: You call yourself a salesman, you son of a b....?

Dave Moss: I don't gotta listen to this s...!

Blake: You certainly don't, pal. 'Cause the good news is you're fired. The bad news is you've got, all you've got, just one week to regain your jobs, starting with tonight.

Starting with tonights sit. Oh, have I got your attention now? Good. 'Cause we're adding a little something to this months sales contest. As you all know, first prize is a Cadillac Eldorado. Anybody wanna see second prize? Second prize's a set of steak knives. Third prize is you're fired.

Do you get the picture? Are you laughing now? You got leads. Mitch and Murray paid good money. Get their names to sell them! You can't close the leads you're given, you can't close s..., you are s..., hit the bricks, pal, and beat it 'cause you're going out!!!

Shelley "The Machine" Levene: The leads are weak.

Blake: The *leads* are weak. F....ng leads are weak? *You're* weak. I've been in this business fifteen years.

Dave Moss: What's your name?

Blake: F... Y..! That's my name!! You know why, Mister? 'Cause you drove a Hyundai to get here tonight, I drove an 80,000 dollar BMW. *That's* my name!! *[To Shelley "The Machine" Levene]* And your name is "you're wanting". And you can't play in a mans' game.

You can't close them. *[At a near whisper]* Then go home and tell your wife your troubles. *[To everyone again]* Because only one thing counts in this life! Get them to sign on the line, which is dotted!

You hear me, you f....ng f....ts? *[Blake flips over a blackboard which has two sets of letters on it: ABC and AIDA.]* A-B-C. A-Always, B-Be, C-Closing. Always be closing! Always be closing!

A-I-D-A. Attention, Interest, Decision, Action. Attention - do I have your attention? Interest - are you interested? I know you are 'cause it's f... or walk.

You close, or you hit the bricks! Decision -- have you made your decision for Christ?!! And action. A-I-D-A.   Get out there!! You got the prospects coming in. You think they came in to get outta the rain? Guys don't walk on the lot 'less he wants to buy. Sitting out there waiting to give you their money! Are you gonna take it? Are you man enough to take it?

Dave Moss: Incredible.

Blake: *[to Moss]* What's the problem, pal? You. Moss. *[Blake sits down.]*

Dave Moss: You're such a hero, you're so rich. How come you're coming down here waste your time with such a bunch of bums?

Blake: You see this watch? *[Blake takes off his gold watch.]* You see this watch?

Dave Moss: Yeah.

Blake: That watch cost more than your car. I made $970,000 last year. How much you make? You see, pal, that's who I am. And you're nothing. Nice guy? I don't give a s.... Good father? F... you, go home and play with your kids!! *[To everyone]* You wanna work here? Close!! *[To George Aaronow]* You think this is abuse? You think this is abuse, you c... sucker?

You can't take this, how can you take the abuse you get on a sit?! You don't like it, leave. I can go out there tonight, the materials you got, make myself $15,000!

Tonight! In two hours! Can you? Can you? Go and do likewise! A-I-D-A!! Get mad! You son of a b.....s! Get mad!! You know what it takes to sell real estate? *[He pulls something out of his brief case. He is holding two brass balls on string]* It takes brass balls to sell real estate. *[He puts them away after a pause.]* Go and do likewise, gents.

The money's out there, you pick it up, it's yours. You don't, I got no sympathy for you. You wanna go out on those sits tonight and close, close, it's yours. If not, you're gonna be shining my shoes.

And you know what you'll be saying, bunch of losers, sitting around in a bar. *[In a mocking weak voice]* "Oh yeah, I used to be a salesman, it's a tough racket." *[He takes out large stack of red index cards tied together with string from his briefcase.]*

These are the new leads. These are the Glengarry leads. And to you, they're gold. And you don't get them. Why? 'Cause to give them to you is just throwing them away. *[He hands the stack to John Williamson.]*

They're for closers. I'd wish you good luck, but you wouldn't know what to do with it if you got it. *[To Moss as he puts on his watch again]*

79

And to answer your question, pal, why am I here?

I came here because Mitch and Murray asked me to, they asked for a favour.

I said the real favour, follow my advice and fire your f....ng ass 'cause a loser is a loser.

2. Boiler room

Seth Davis is a college dropout running an illegal casino from his rented apartment.

Driven by his domineering fathers disapproval at his illegitimate existence and his desire for serious wealth, Seth suddenly finds himself seduced by the opportunity to interview as a trainee stock broker from recent acquaintance Greg (Nicky Katt).

Walking into the offices of JT Marlin, a small time brokerage firm on the outskirts of New York - Seth gets an aggressive cameo performance from Jay (Ben Affleck) that sets the tone for a firm clearly placing money above all else. Seths' fractured relationship with his father and flirtatious glances from love interest Abbie (Nia Long) are enough to keep Seth motivated in his new found career.

As he begins to excel and develop a love for the hard sale and high commission, a few chance encounters leads Seth to question the legitimacy of the firms operations placing him once again at odds with his father and what remains of his morality.

My favourite lines are the following:

Man on phone: Take me off your list.

Seth Davis: Fine, fine. I'm gonna take you off my list of successful people today. **Jim Young:** And there is no such thing as a "No" sale call. A sale is made on every call you make. Either you sell the client some stock or he sells you a reason he can't. Either way a sale is made, the only question is who is gonna close? You or him? Now be relentless, that's it, I'm done.

Jim Young: They say money can't buy happiness? Look at the f....ng smile on my face. Ear to ear, baby.

Jim Young: Anybody who tells you money is the root of all evil doesn't have any.

Seth Davis: What do you mean, you're gonna pass. Alan, the only people making money passing are NFL quarterbacks and I don't see a number on your back.

Greg Weinstein: Don't pitch the b...h

Chris Varick: Hey, kid, get the f... out of here.

Seth Davis: I read this article a while back that said that Microsoft employs more millionaire secretaries than any other company in the world.

They took stock options over Christmas bonuses. It was a good move. I remember there was this picture, of one of the groundskeepers next to his Ferrari.

Blew my mind. You see s... like that, and it just plants seeds, makes you think it's possible, even easy.

And then you turn on the TV, and there's just more of it

The $87 million lottery winner, that kid actor that just made $20 million off his last movie, that internet stock that shot through the roof, you could have made millions if you had just gotten in early, and that's exactly what I wanted to do: get in.

I didn't want to be an innovator any more, I just wanted to make the quick and easy buck, I just wanted in. The Notorious BIG said it best: "Either you're slingin' crack-rock, or you've got a wicked jump-shot". Nobody wants to work for it anymore.

There's no honour in taking that after school job at Mickey Dee's, honour's in the dollar, kid. So I went the white boy way of slinging crack-rock: I became a stock broker.

Broker: I know you're not standing on your front porch with a bag of money waiting for me to call you. But I'm not some eighteen year old selling a cure for AIDS.

I'm forty-six years old, I have twenty-two years market experience and I know this business. So pick up your skirt, grab your balls, and let's go make some money

Jim Young: There's an important phrase that we use here, and think it's time that you all learned it. Act as if. You understand what that means? Act as if you are the f....ng president of this firm. Act as if you got a 9 inch c..k Okay? Act as if.

Seth Davis: It's strange to think how that knock changed everything, everything, hey don't get me wrong here, I don't believe in fate, I believe in odds.

Greg Weinstein: Don't you have a canoli you can stick in your mouth?

Chris Varick: Don't you have a menorah you could shove up your ass?

Jim Young: You want details? Fine. I drive a Ferrari, 355 Cabriolet. What's up? I have a ridiculous house in the South Fork. I have every toy you could possibly imagine. And best of all kids, I am liquid.

Richie: Get the f... out of here before I put you in a mayonnaise jar.

Richie: When was the last time you closed something huh? You couldn't close a f....ng window you moron!

Greg Weinstein: I hope this is better than the last batch of s... you gave me. Produced more wood than Ron Jeremy. I don't want you to yell, "Reco!" anymore. Know what you should yell? "Timber!" Yeah, Mr F....ng wood. I hear you f....ng makin' your calls. It's bull...., all right? I mean if you want them off the phone so bad, why don't you just hang up? You should get them excited. You know, excited? They should beg for a broker on the first call.

Jim Young: You become an employee of this firm, you will make your first million within three years. I'm gonna repeat that - you will make a million dollars.

Greg Weinstein: Hang up. Hang up the phone.

Seth Davis: Thank you. That's nice for you to do that for me.

Greg Weinstein: First of all, there's gonna be a lot of these regardless of how good you, are but you happen to suck big fat ass rhinoceros d...

Seth Davis: Well, thank you. That's confidence inspiring.

Seth Davis: I had a very strong work ethic. The problem was my ethics in work.

Greg Weinstein: Now there are two rules you have to remember as a trainee, number one, we don't pitch the bi... here.

Seth Davis: What?

Greg Weinstein: We don't sell stock to women. I don't care who it is, we don't do it. Nancy Sinatra calls, you tell her you're sorry.

They're a constant pain in the ass and you're never going to hear the end of it alright?

They're going to call you every f....ng day wanting to know why the stock is dropping and God forbid the stock should go up; you're going to hear from them every fifteen minutes.

It's just not worth it, don't pitch the b...h!

Comments by Vefa Enver:

I haven't known anyone who has achieved for the sake of achieving. You either have the motivation to put all your heart and effort into whatever you are doing to reach the top or you live a life of "almost".

Almost you made it, almost you got it, almost you earned it. But we all know almost doesn't count. Sometimes all we need is a little push or maybe someone sticking around who truly believes in us.

The Inch by Inch speech which is made by Al Pacino in the movie "Any Given Sunday" is quite a good example of motivational approach.

Any Given Sunday released in 1999 was written by Daniel Pyne and John Logan, directed by Oliver Stone.

Al Pacino's Inch by Inch Speech

I don't know what to say really. Three minutes to the biggest battle of our professional lives all comes down to today.

Either we heal as a team or we are going to crumble.

Inch by inch, play by play 'till we're finished. We are in hell right now, gentlemen, believe me and we can stay here and get the s..t kicked out of us or we can fight our way back into the light.

We can climb out of hell. One inch at a time.

Now I can't do it for you. I'm too old. I look around and I see these young faces and I think I mean... I made every wrong choice a middle age man could make. I uh.... I pissed away all my money, believe it or not. I chased off anyone who has ever loved me. And lately, I can't even stand the face I see in the mirror.

You know when you get old in life things get taken from you.

That's, that's part of life. But, you only learn that when you start losing stuff. You find out that life is just a game of inches. So is football.

Because in either game, life or football, the margin for error is so small.

I mean one half step too late or too early you don't quite make it. One half second too slow or too fast and you don't quite catch it.

The inches we need are everywhere around us. They are in every break of the game every minute, every second. On this team, we fight for that inch.

On this team, we tear ourselves, and everyone around us to pieces for that inch. We CLAW with our finger nails for that inch.

Cause we know when we add up all those inches that's going to make the f....ng difference between WINNING and LOSING, between LIVING and DYING.

I'll tell you this, in any fight it is the guy who is willing to die who is going to win that inch.

And I know if I am going to have any life anymore it is because, I am still willing to fight, and die for that inch, because that is what LIVING is. The six inches in front of your face.

Now I can't make you do it. You gotta look at the guy next to you. Look into his eyes.

Now I think you are going to see a guy who will go that inch with you. You are going to see a guy who will sacrifice himself for this team because he knows when it comes down to it, you are gonna do the same thing for him.

That's a team gentlemen, and either we heal now, as a team, or we will die as individuals.

That's football guys. That's all it is.

Now, what are you gonna do?

Chapter 7: The Young Entrepreneur

"The entrepreneur always searches for change, responds to it, and exploits it as an opportunity."

Peter Drucker

I met my wife Jamie in 2006. We got married that same year. At that stage I was heading up the media-buying team at the company I was employed at.

I was twenty-six years old, earning big money and my plan for how life should be was well on track.

I never saw it coming as everything was going so well. We got the news at a company breakfast that a merger was taking place and we were facing retrenchment. Our department was first! I had just got married and Jamie was pregnant. I went into a panic...

I accepted a voluntary package and I entered the world of entrepreneurship. These days are covered in my second book "The Next Best Thing". I never worked for a boss again. At twenty-seven, Thaamir Moerat the businessman was officially born!

I love being an entrepreneur! I love the thrill of start-ups. I am a real hunter, I hate farming! I will always setup, retain my shareholding and move on!

It is what I am, it is what I do. I get bored quickly. It is an asset and a liability, strength and weakness. My mother always said that my ambition is going kill me someday. I can't stop pushing; I can't stop the fear of having to go back to that dark place when my dad lost everything.

I can't ever put my kids through that. I programmed myself to always be hungry, to always be driven.

I will always hunt... The entrepreneur in me will never rest.

I had the priveledge of meeting Nelson Mandela. I spent five hours at his house in Cape Town after being the youngest finalist in Mr SA in the year 2000. I took it for granted. At twenty years old, I was a kid and did not know the magnitude of the situation. I am honoured to be able to say that I had lunch with this great man and that he requested my company.

Mandela was arguably the worlds most celebrated, recognised and popular leader. He was an anti-apartheid revolutionary, politician and philanthropist who served as President of South Africa from 1994 to 1999 and passed away in December 2013. He lived, shared and encouraged great lessons that every entrepreneur can and should use.

Nelson Mandelas' fight and ultimate victory over apartheid was an inspiration to many people around the world and in South Africa.

Mandela once said: "It is never my custom to use words lightly. If twenty seven years in prison have done anything to us, it was to use the silence of solitude to make us understand how precious words are and how real speech is in its impact on the way people live and die."

Here are six inspirational quotes shared by Nelson Mandela that can impact your life and your business positively:

1. "It always seems impossible until it's done."

Skeptics will always say to you: "That's impossible". Your friends will, your family will, your ex-bosses will but those who have built successful companies know the truth about the word "impossible".

"Nothing is impossible; the word itself says 'I'mpossible."

- Audrey Hepburn

"Progress is impossible without change, and those who cannot

change their minds cannot change anything."

- George Bernard Shaw

"Impossible is a word to be found only in the dictionary of fools."

- Napoleon Bonaparte

"Impossible is just a big word thrown around by small men who find it easier to live in the world they've been given than to explore the power they have to change it. Impossible is not a fact. It's an opinion. Impossible is not a declaration. It's a dare. Impossible is potential. Impossible is temporary. Impossible is nothing."

- Muhammad Ali

"The impossible becomes possible if only your mind believes it."

- Chris Bradford

2. "Do not judge me by my successes, judge me by how many times I fell down and got back up again."

I hope that by reading my books you will see that I have fallen so many times but every time I get back up. It is part and parcel of being an entrepreneur. If you cannot handle that, get a 9-5 job and make someone else rich.

3. "Everyone can rise above their circumstances and achieve success if they are dedicated to and passionate about what they do."

Any line of business that you are in, any sports organisation or charity club you belong to, you will inevitably hear someone tell you the importance of dedication and passion.

Dedication equips you for the road ahead while passion inspires you to go the extra mile when others would likely tell you to "stop what you are doing" or "give up".

Many of us will never go through what Mandela has gone through or even come close to his struggles but without dedication and passion, success is so much harder to achieve.

You need lots of dedication and passion to succeed!

And here I am not referring to passion fruit! lol

4. "There is no passion to be found in playing small, in settling for a life that is less than the one you are capable of living."

What is your real potential? What is your "Good enough barometer"? You are capable of much more than you ever think or believe you are. My third book is all about pushing that barometer! Challenge yourself!

'Cause good enough never is, good enough doesn't cut it!

5. "Difficulties break some men but make others."

Starting any new business venture is full of small victories and lots of challenges. Yet what truly distinguishes a winner from the pack is the will to keep on going. To never give up!

Learning to overcome business challenges is part of the course of entrepreneurship.

From competing against big companies and learning how to get your brand out there, to building a winning company culture and hiring the right staff, these obstacles should always be seen as opportunities and should be welcomed and defeated.

Just like Mandela saw every challenge as an obstacle to be beaten! Winners thrive on challenges…

6. "I learned that courage was not the absence of fear, but the triumph over it. The brave man is not he who does not feel afraid, but he who conquers that fear."

Before pursueing your brightest and greatest business concept or trying to get your first customer and while preparing your business plan and projections or exploring new markets and opportunities you will come face to face with fear many times, over and over again. So, before you master any other skill, master the art of overcoming your fears and insecurities.

"There is no illusion greater than fear." - *Lao Tzu*

Rest in Peace Madiba. You will always be my endless source of inspiration. *1918-2013*

At first publication of this book in 2013, I have interests in seven different companies in four different industries and three more ventures in the pipeline.

I have dedicated much of my next book to this topic so I do not want to ponder too much on my days in the industry as an owner.

I am an entrepreneur, no doubt about that!

I love to quote people who are doing it for themselves and the Americans seem to be in front in the pecking order of young millionaires.

I will close with 16 quotes from Americas coolest young entrepreneurs.

Start-up Secrets:

Useful Tips from Americas Coolest Young Entrepreneurs!

Stick With It

"Start-ups don't die, they commit suicide. In other words, 90 percent of start-ups fail because the founders get bored, discouraged, or something else and they move on to other things, not because of some catastrophe. No matter how dark it is today, things will always better tomorrow."

Justin Kan, Justin.TV

Simplify Your Mission

"I would encourage other entrepreneurs to spend a lot of time boiling down what their business is, what it does, and what it represents. If you nail down a 60 to 90 second synopsis, that will pay a lot of dividends throughout the life of your business."

Eric Koger, ModCloth

Ditch Your Safety Net

"As a senior at Babson, I lined up a job at Goldman Sachs. I thought I was pretty smart since this would give me a backup if IdeaPaint wasn't working out. Looking back now, I realized that having that in hand was a reason not to push harder and higher. The day before the job started, I told them I wanted to pursue IdeaPaint. They thought I was crazy, but I think it has worked out pretty well."

John Goscha, IdeaPaint

Exceed Expectations

"We knew we only had one shot at this, so there was nothing throughout our start-up that we didn't purposely over deliver on, from the way we pitched our distributors and investors to the way we rolled out in the market. If you always over-deliver, it is going to draw attention and you will likely be successful."

Jeff Avallon, IdeaPaint

Do More With Less

"That is something we've definitely exemplified. When you have limited resources, you constantly have to be really creative about the way you can make things work."

Morgan Newman, IdeaPaint

Have a Money Plan

"We are no longer in an era where potential investors or acquirers go after companies who focus on their user count."

Kyle Vogt, Justin.TV

Be Nimble

"The landscape no longer changes every two, three, four years like it did in 2002. If you're not quick on your toes, you will miss opportunities."

Tristan Harris, Apture

You Can't Mask Mediocrity

"Steve Martin said it best. Be undeniably good. No marketing effort or social media buzzword can be a substitute for that."

Anthony Volodkin, Hype Machine

Don't Go It Alone

"Surround yourself with an awesome team because you're going to need them to overcome all the obstacles that come with starting a company. Lots of people have great ideas that they try to tackle by themselves, but

I think it's almost impossible to do everything by yourself."

Emily Olson, Foodzie

Do Your Homework

"Be really clear about the assumptions you're making about the business you're going into, and check those assumptions as quickly as you can, whether it's building a prototype and testing it with people, or just talking to other people in the industry."

Can Sar, Apture

Send In the Geeks

"Starting with a highly technical founding team is the key to being a flexible web technology company."

Michael Seibel, Justin.TV

Be Prepared

Educate yourself on whatever you're going into. If you don't know what you're doing, people will take advantage of you. Exercise your right to negotiate, especially as a woman; don't be afraid to walk away from an opportunity that you don't think is right for you; and be realistic about your budget. Figure out how much you need to save and then try to keep yourself on a strict budget."

Kyle Smitley, Barley & Birch

Stay Genuine

"Do what you know and love! It will resonate with your customers, employees, and potential investors. And make all the hard work worthwhile."

Susan Gregg Koger, ModCloth

Do What You Love

"It's a common saying, but vitally important. The more you enjoy your job, the easier it is to work, and that's important, especially when starting up your own company. You will be amazed at the amount of time and energy it will take to make your company successful."

Jamail Larkins, Ascension Aircraft

Don't Manage Angry

"Be as stern as you need to be, but nothing good comes from you bringing your lack of emotional control into the work."

Adam Rich, Thrillist

Don't Be Afraid

"If you have an idea, do it. When you're in your 20s or 30s, that's the time where you can be aggressive and be a risk-taker. That's the beauty of youth."

Michael Nardy, Electronic Payments

I have a saying: "First do what makes you rich and THEN you will be able to do what you love!" There are different schools of thoughts but most believe that you must do what you love and success will come. I disagree and again, this is just my opinion. I started my first sales call centre when I was twenty-seven and six years later, I can honestly say that I hate the industry but I am good at it... the best! At first publication of this book at year end 2013, I have interests in four different call centre annuity products all running smoothly. (More about that in: "The next Best Thing.") I worked hard at what I was good at for six years and today, I am doing what I like, what I want to do. I am writing, presenting, speaking, modelling etc. And money is not the deciding factor for what I do with my time. I paid my dues and I am reaping the rewards. (More about this in "Good Enough Doesn't Cut It".)

Comments by Vefa Enver:

If Ludwig van Beethovens' Symphony 9 was completed in 1824 when he was **completely deaf**, which is considered to be one of the masterpieces in classical music history, what physical and practical impossibilities are we talking about?

The only and the greatest obstacle in front of ones achievment is probably the person himself. You might not have money to pay the bills and you know what neither did J.K Rowling - the writer of the Harry Potter series.

"We were as skint as you can be without being homeless and at that point I was definitely clinically depressed."

"That was characterised by a numbness, a coldness and an inability to believe you will feel happy again. All the colour drained out of life" says Rowling.

After hitting an all-time low she rised right up to the sky at an amazing speed. It doesn't matter how deep you fall but how high you bounce back.

Who would have thought she would become a worldwide famous writer of bestselling books? Miracles happen but only when you put faith, effort and sweat into whatever you are doing. Without having written a book, she wouldn't have become a famous author. Each step takes you to your goal as long as you don't give up.

Remember God helps those who helps themselves.

Chapter 8: Mamma I sold you

"The ultimate measure of a man is not where he stands in moments of comfort and convenience, but where he stands at times of challenge."

Martin Luther King, Jr.

I made the call that was about to change my life... as I was facing rejection all day I told myself that this was my last attempt and if I didn't close this sale I wasn't going to come back the next day. I was about to give up.

I can honestly say that it was sheer hunger and desperation that pushed me to make that sale and even though I tried to repeat the intensity and sheer passion of that call I could never get it right as I was never in the frame of mind that I was in at that moment of my life ever again. I can't recall the exact time but it was dark outside and the call centre was empty.

It was just Danjoe and I. Sales manager and his prodigy.

Danjoe was just sitting there watching me, like a rugby coach watching his star player from the grand stand. He was rooting for me; I could see it in his eyes.

I can honestly say that anyone who is not in sales cannot fully understand the impact that a good sales manager can have on his troops. As just a mere look boosted my confidence so much, it felt almost as if he was with me on that call.

I had to clear the mechanism, as the fact that I did not have petrol money to get back home and didn't have any money for food was still lingering above me like a dark cloud. All my doubts and insecurities came back to me at that point. I was not only pitching to Mama. She was not the only person on the other side of the line.

I was pitching against time, I was pitching against all my fears, I was pitching against all my demons, I was pitching against my family that wasn't there for us, I was pitching against the wealthy arrogant boy that I used to be who thought life was always going to be a fairytale. I was pitching to my mom. I was pitching against my dad, who wasn't man enough to ask all those people who owed him money to please pay him back even if it was just bit by bit so that we could eat. I was pitching against life, I was pitching against destiny. How ironic that when the call was answered I heard a voice that said: "Hello you're speaking to Destiny, but you can call me Mama".

At that moment I knew that God had a better plan for me. I decided to go for it!

Everything just came to me. Everything I heard all day from the seasoned agents came back to me. I was using opening techniques I was yet to learn. I was handling objections like a seasoned veteran. Every question that Mama threw at me I answered with confidence.

This was going to be it. This was going to be the birth of a salesman. As my pitch progressed, I could see Danjoe get excited and pointing to me to stand up. Later in my career, I learnt that motion creates emotion. It's not only about how well you speak but how well you move while speaking. All great sales people have that gift. They know how to move, they know how to act. If you can't act you can't sell.

I did everything I possibly could to get the sale. Just as I was about to close, Mama threw me a curve ball. She told me that she did not need this cover. But instead of accepting rejection, like I did all day, I pulled out my chair, sat down, told Mama to sit down too, looked at Danjoe and placed my call on speaker. Like a real coach, Danjoe stood up and made his way to my desk.

He guided me through my first close. He told me to ask her if she had children and to pitch her on her insecurities and love for her children. She told me she has four sons. But the youngest one was her favourite. I can't remember if I heard correctly but it sounded like she said his name was Shapping. At that moment, something clicked. All the closing techniques that I was still to learn, that I never even knew existed came to me. As part of my product that I was selling was anti retroviral and South Africa has a high HIV fatality rate, I asked her what Shapping was doing. She said he was outside playing soccer in the street.

I said to her: "Shapping! He's playing in the street? What if Shapping falls and cuts his knee and his friend also has bloody knees and their blood mixes. He can get AIDS if his friend is infected!"

Mama jumped out of her chair and shouted: "My baby can get AIDS!?"

I said: "Yes Mama, but if you take this cover, should that happen he will get free anti retroviral treatment".

Mama replied by saying: "Give me this cover!"

And that was music to my ears!!!!

Danjoe, leaped so high into the air he almost knocked his head against the roof. I continued to take down her details. When I got to her bank details she told me that she did not have it with her and that I should hold on, she will walk to the ATM and get a statement.

She begged me not to drop the phone.

I held on and told her: "Mama I will walk with you".

After fifteen minutes of hearing Mama breathe heavily on the other side of the phone, she got to the ATM and gave me her account number. I did the declaration and Mama was sold!

I was officially a salesman. Words cannot explain the feeling of utter accomplishment when a salesman makes his first real sale. Few can remember it. I'm lucky that I remember the day I sold Mama.

I climbed the ranks so quickly after that call and received a promotion after one month. Although I was still on the phones, I had a team of 12 agents to manage.

Recognising when to promote a sales rep is very important as that extra responsibility and recognition can lead to extra drive which means more sales for your company.

Here are the seven signs to look for when considering if a sales rep should be promoted or not:

Consistently exceeding sales targets:

In any sales game, fulfilling your sales job description is exceeding your minimum sales targets. Yet, to get promoted, the sales rep must do it consistently and not just occasionally. He must perform month in and month out.

Put in the extra effort:

The best sales reps are the ones who make their target while helping you. They take on the responsibility for training, coaching and mentoring new reps effortlessly and with pleasure.

Somehow they figure out how to do it while remaining on target and making it look easy.

Be the informal leader of the pack:

Watch for the rest of the team turning to this person when no one is watching! They don't promote themselves as know-it-alls', yet they get all the questions thrown their way. In sales meetings, others want their opinions on matters.

They don't usually voice them without being asked first. People ask them specifically most of the time. Their views and opinions almost always sway the decision.

Does something of value all the time:

The promotable sales rep does something valuable for his teammates without being asked. It could be by going on a sales call, helping with a sales strategy or running a sales meeting.

They consistently take the lead and help others yet they do it without any real benefit to them.

They display constructive criticism:

They never complain and the side shows don't bother them! They provide professional, mature constructive criticism. Things aren't always right but how you voice your opinion counts.

No excuses:

You never have to make an excuse for this person. They always get it done no matter what the challenge or obstacle. You rely on them consistently without defending their actions. They are your go-to-men in a time of crisis.

Easy to coach and eager to learn:

They actually listen, take notes and practise what you teach them. This means that your coaching and one-on-one feedback help them sell.

A good sales manger should learn to recognise these traits, but recognising these signs in your sales reps takes time and only really seasoned sales managers notice these signs quickly.

You must frequently attend sales meetings or go out to see them in action.

Depending on your sales channel, try to attend customer meetings with them. If you just listen to your second-in-charge, the critical interactions will be missed and the signs of a promotable rep will be lost.

Unfortunately, this happens way too often.

When it does, the sales rep that sucks up to the boss is promoted above the best ones.

Don't let this happen to you and don't let it happen in your sales organisation.

Take the time to know who your best people are and give credit (promotion) where necessary.

After all, people work for people and not for companies.

Chapter 9: Tribute to Danjoe

"Stay Hungry. Stay Driven. Like The Wolf!"

Duran Duran

We have already established that there was a time in my life, years ago that I was in the depths of a major depression.

At twenty, my father had gone bankrupt a year or two before and my life as I knew it was in turmoil. I fell into call centre sales as I always had a "mouth" on me. Besides, the only office jobs available for matriculants or varsity drop-outs was sales in a call centre back then, as I was not prepared to waiter or dance on a bar (yet).

Sales came naturally to me and after closing "Mama" I just got better and better! I was doing very well, breaking all the hourly, daily and weekly sales records and was on my way to becoming the top salesperson in the companies history.

But new sales had slowed down a little, and I didn't have my usual number of policies on the board. So, I wasn't as busy as usual. As my activity slowed, I began to worry about my stats and my sales territory. My doubts, insecurities and concerns increased to the point where I had thought myself into a real depression, stuck on that hopeless question that I never ask myself - "What's the use of trying?"

The more negative my thoughts became, the less energy and drive I had. My lack of enthusiasm led to fewer and fewer sales calls, which of course, led to fewer numbers and that led to more depressing thoughts.

I was caught in a powerful downward spiral. I went from 16 a day to 10 to 8 to 4…

It was then that I caught a glimpse of what a professional sales manager is like.

Danjoe Horn was my boss. One of the best leaders and sales managers I have ever had the honour of working for. He could see the symptoms of my negative mindset spilling over into everything I was doing.

So Danjoe intervened. He arranged to have lunch with me, and listened patiently as I told him about my problems, my doubts, my insecurities, my concerns, and my lack of activity.

Finally, after I was done thinking up all the excuses for not producing and dumped all my depression and negative thoughts on him, he looked me straight in the eye and said, with all the authority of someone who is absolutely sure of what they are saying, "Thaamir, that's enough!"

I was dump struck! Stunned! I thought to myself: what the f...! I was expecting empathy, an understanding shoulder to cry on.

Instead, I got a simple, straightforward mandate. Danjoe knew me well enough to cut through all the rubbish and come right to the heart of the matter.

He said: "That's enough. That's enough feeling sorry for yourself Thaamir. That's enough thinking all these negative thoughts all the time. That's enough lying back and not working as hard as you're used to. Stop it. You're f.....g better than all of this. Stop it right now, today, and get your ass back to work".

He saw my situation clearly. And he provided me the direction I needed.

That conversation turned me around. I left my depression and negativity at that lunch table and went back to the phones with a renewed sense of the possible, energised and ready to hunt again.

Five years later as I grew in my career, receiving the highest sales accolades in two companies and heading up departments, our paths crossed again as business associates. More on that in my third book titled "Good Enough Doesn't Cut It".

What made the difference in my performance was the skilful intervention of a direct, confident and professional sales manager.

He made the difference in my career that day. He indirectly led me to my current practice.

It's entirely possible that I would not be doing what I do now, speaking and consulting with sales forces around the country, writing sales training books and manuals and be the go-to-guy for new and exciting call centre products (I currently have five) if it weren't for his timely intervention.

All of us have become what we are, not entirely, but partially because of the impact other people have had on us, some positive and some negative. They all moulded us. Everyone we have had experiences with in our lives.

A professional sales manager is gifted with a very rare and precious opportunity, the opportunity to play a pivotal role in the lives of his subordinates. I so value the role that Danjoe played in my career, that this, the second last chapter on my first sales book must read: "Finally, I must make special acknowledgement to the contribution made by Danjoe Horn to my career, the best sales manager I ever worked for. It was Danjoe who, years ago, urged me to "write the book" not with words, but actions that he himself did not really know he was doing".

So what does this have to do with being a "Professional Sales Manager?" During my 9+ years of sales experience and three years of experience as a sales director, consultant and sales trainer, I've encountered many sales managers and leaders. Very few of them have been good, many mediocre. But Danjoe was the best sales manager I ever met, partnered with and worked for.

He served as a "Sales" role model for me. I learnt a number of lessons from him.

An excellent sales manager, like a great rugby coach, is ultimately measured by his numbers and nothing else. It doesn't matter how good he is with people or how his players respect or like him, if year after year he produces a losing team.

It is the same with a sales manager. Ultimately, an excellent sales manager produces excellent numbers for his company. He puts the money in the companies' bank account. In the five years that I worked for and with Danjoe, my own intellectual capacity grew from mediocre to excellent.

Danjoe was great at one of the key competencies of the professional sales manager... he had an eye for talent. He knew how to hire good people. After all, he hired me!

A professional sales manager understands the importance of hiring, is always busy recruiting in order to keep the pipeline of prospective salespeople full, and spares no expense to make sure the person he hires meets all the necessary criteria.

With all the time he took to make sure he was hiring the right person, Danjoe confided in me one day that, "It is more important to fire well than it is to hire well."

He went on to explain that hiring salespeople is an extremely difficult task, and that even the best sales managers fail at it all the time. Therefore, it was important to recognise your mistake quickly, and act decisively to fix it.

A professional sales manager also understands that when it is clear that a salesperson is not right for the job, he acts quickly, kindly, and decisively to terminate the individual, allowing both the individual and the company an opportunity to find a better match. Acting quickly to terminate a salesperson who isn't working out is both good business as well as good ethics.

Understanding that he works only through his salespeople, and that he has the opportunity to make a great impact on his staff, a professional sales manager makes it his business to know his people.

Danjoe spent days with me when we became associates, talking not only about business, but also working at understanding the person I was as well. He'd arrange to meet me for breakfast or lunch regularly, even if he wasn't spending the day with me.

He wanted to get to know my wife as well, and paid close attention to her opinions.

I could never stop by the office without being expected to sit in his office and talk about things like rugby or a good movie he had seen.

Because he took the time to get to know me and what makes me tick, he was equipped with the knowledge of exactly how to best manage and drive me and he always saw the potential in me.

He was always ready to correct me when necessary. In the first year of my employment, I was earning the reputation among the customer support and QA people of being difficult, a conceited hotshot. I was a sales superstar who didn't take their feelings into consideration and always had a lot to say about them not bringing in the cash and just being there doing a cushy job. Danjoe let me know that my ways needed to change.

At first, I didn't pay much attention. My numbers on the board were too good for anybody to be concerned as in sales it is all about the numbers.

So Danjoe let me know a second time that I was going to have to change. The situation went so far, that the QA operations manager was pushing for me to get fired!

Guided by his firm hand, I swallowed my pride, adopted a more humble attitude, and bought all the QA's a gift. I ended up being best friends with the head of the quality assurance department and we worked well together to get my quality up to scratch.

A professional sales manager always guides and corrects his charges in order to help them achieve their full potential at all costs.

Danjoe never stopped learning or reading sales books. He would often tell me about seminars he had attended, books he'd read, or ideas he'd picked up by talking with other sales people.

He knew that he would never "know it all". So it is with every professional sales manager in the industry. You want to call yourself a real professional sales manager? Never stop learning!

Understand that you have a challenge to continuously grow and improve, to learn more and become better at your job. Sales management isn't just a job; it's a challenge of a lifetime of learning and improvement.

Understand that a professional sales manager is only as good as his team and vice versa.

He is only successful when his team is successful; an excellent sales manager supports, encourages and gives his sales people the credit, like Danjoe always did.

I am so driven right now it's not even funny!!!

Want to excel as a sales manager? Want to be a true professional leader? Look at your job as a unique opportunity to impact others, to select, correct, support, coach and encourage your salespeople to achieve your companies' objectives by becoming a positive force in their lives. It's not just a job, it's a bloody mission!

Stay Hungry, always be driven, set the example, lead through people and perhaps, one day, fifteen years from now, someone will write about you.

Danjoe, I salute you!

After Danjoe and I parted, life hit me hard… AGAIN!

With 20 000 Rand left in my bank account and two million Rand in debt, I went into my second depression. I met a guy called Paul Johnson who became my biggest test in life (Later I would find out that it was a fake name).

I started doubting myself again and even told my wife that I have forgotten how to make money, until I decided it's time to do: "The Next Best Thing".

In life, as in sales, always do the next best thing…

That said, as I conclude my story for "Mama I Sold You", the next two books in this series titled "The Next Best Thing" and "Good Enough Doesn't Cut It" will continue with my story.

Work Hard - Live Hard - Sell Hard - Play Hard!!!

Comments by Vefa Enver:

"Anyone who wants to sell you overnight success or wealth is not interested in your success; they are interested in your money."- Bo Bennett

Success is not a destination but a life long journey, a way of living because it is more difficult to stay on top than to get there.

Before meeting my dear friend Thaamir, I was not the least interested in sales and marketing.

Being a novelist I might still not be quite interested in "selling hard" but very much in the amazing story behind it.

I believe that everyone who reads this book, whether in sales business or not, will find a lesson or advice which will be great help on their journey of success.

And I know for sure that after having finished reading the last page of the book, being as inspired as me, you will have a different approach towards success and failure.

Contrary to popular belief success is not about being perfect but determined and open to constant learning.

We all have the will but few of us have the courage and ambition to stand up and try again each time we fall down.

Success is falling nine times and getting up ten.

There are only two ways to live your life.One is as though nothing is a miracle. The other is as though everything is a miracle, said Albert Einstein.

Call it being optimistic or even romantic I firmly believe in the latter.

Have faith in yourself and let this book show you the way and you will see that any goal is attainable.

Chapter 10: Conclusion

"Now this is not the end. It is not even the beginning of the end. But it is, perhaps, the end of the beginning."

Winston Churchill

At first publication of this book I have been selling for fifteen years.

During these years, I learned as much as I could about the sales game and kept growing. It was my trial and error period and I was having the time of my life!

So many people crossed my path and I was fortunate enough to have great mentors, some good and some bad. I never stopped learning and started building up my sales library.

A great sales person is a student, always learning, always hungry for more sales knowledge. I was hungry, on top of my game and living the good life. I met my wife Jamie, we had two daughters, I bought new cars, went on holidays… Life was GREAT!

Until I was tested again...

I hope you have enjoyed reading my first sales book as much as I have enjoyed writing it. I must make special mention of my co-writer, Turkish novelist Vefa Enver, who helped me and guided me through my first experience as a writer.

Your expertise was invaluable and I look forward to writing many more with you.

To my wife Jamie, I know it's not easy being married to a guy whose happiness largely depends on his bank balance.

Thank you for understanding and always motivating me. "Behind every successful man is a woman driving him" This quote was written for you...

To my children: Armani, Isra and Dastan Cruz.

You bring purpose to my life and a major part of why I am so driven is because I never want to see you go through what I did.

To everyone who played a part in moulding me, knowingly or not, I salute you and wish you all the success in the world.

In closing, I do not claim to know it all; on the contrary I am just a student of life and the sales game which I made my profession.

My books are my views based on my experiences and it is not intended to harm anyone. Learn from it, as I did... Take in what you can and always remember to Sell Hard!

My story does not end here... it starts here.

"We learn something from everyone who passes through our lives. Some lessons are painful, some are painless, but all are priceless!"

Çok Çalış. İyi Yaşa. İyi Sat. Çok Eğlen!